Piece & Love

11 FUN, EASY-TO-SEW QUILTS

Diane Brinton and Audrey Mann
of THE CLOTH PARCEL

Martingale®
Create with Confidence

Piece & Love: 11 Fun, Easy-to-Sew Quilts
© 2022 by Diane Brinton and Audrey Mann

Martingale®
18939 120th Ave NE, Suite 101
Bothell, WA 98011-9511 USA
ShopMartingale.com

Printed in Hong Kong
27 26 25 24 23 22   8 7 6 5 4 3 2 1

Library of Congress Cataloging-in-Publication Data is available upon request.

ISBN: 978-1-68356-178-1

MISSION STATEMENT

We empower makers who use fabric and yarn to make life more enjoyable.

CREDITS

PUBLISHER AND
CHIEF VISIONARY OFFICER
Jennifer Erbe Keltner

CONTENT DIRECTOR
Karen Costello Soltys

DESIGN MANAGER
Adrienne Smitke

TECHNICAL EDITOR
Elizabeth Beese

PRODUCTION MANAGER
Regina Girard

COPY EDITOR
Durby Peterson

PHOTOGRAPHERS
Adam Albright
Brent Kane

ILLUSTRATOR
Sandy Loi

SPECIAL THANKS
Photography for this book was taken at the homes of Libby Warnken of Ankeny, Iowa, and Tracy Fish of Kenmore, Washington.

Contents

Introduction

Welcome to our colorful world of modern large-scale design! Make a big impact with a giant heart, cupcake, star, and more. Each quilt uses several blocks to form a single object. Use eye-catching, bright colors on a muted background to make each of these 11 quilt designs shine.

Create a focal point with In Bloom, a smaller, cheerful wall hanging, or a grand sunset with Sundown, a twin-size design. All of the other project sizes fall somewhere between these, but the beauty they all share is that they're quick and easy to complete. Use your imagination to find new ways to display each quilt. Wall hangings can also work as table runners, and twin-size bed quilts are great for throws!

The designs are perfect for the confident beginner looking to try some new techniques with blocks in manageable sizes. For example, give paper piecing a whirl with just a couple of blocks in Paint Box (page 75), try a bit of appliqué in Sundown (page 27), or use templates to piece a few blocks for Sprinkles (page 13).

We've included a quilt for nearly every season to celebrate year-round. You'll enjoy making each of these in a variety of different color schemes, perfect for your home or for gifting to friends and family. Follow the guidelines for light, medium, and dark value fabrics, but inject your personality and creativity by choosing your own color palette.

Time to get piecing!

Diane & Audrey

Piece & Love

Set colorful triangles of varied hues into a faceted heart that sparkles against a calming striped background. This modern stunner is perfect in any colorway. Pick fabrics with a wide color range and stick to small prints for best results.

FINISHED QUILT: 58" × 58" | **FINISHED BLOCK: 5¾" × 5¾"**

Materials

Yardage is based on 42"-wide fabric.

- 20 fat eighths, 9" × 21", of assorted prints ranging from light to dark for heart; sort fabrics into colors 1–20*
- 1 yard of white solid for background stripe
- 2⅜ yards of gray solid for background stripe and binding
- 3⅝ yards of fabric for backing
- 64" × 64" square of batting

*Label your fabrics as shown in the fabric key below so you can follow a color progression when laying out the quilt. We used a loosely organized rainbow (from pink to dark blue) that generally goes from light to dark. For interest, we included a few lighter fabrics (such as fabrics 3, 7, and 11) out of order and swapped a few fabrics in neighboring colors (such as green and blue).

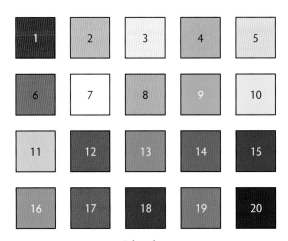

Fabric key

Cutting

All measurements include ¼" seam allowances.

From *each* of the assorted prints, cut:
2 squares, 7½" × 7½" (40 total); cut the squares into quarters diagonally to yield 8 small triangles (160 total; 8 will be extra) **Note:** If you prefer to use precuts, you'll need 80 squares, 5" × 5"; cut them in half diagonally. Using 5" squares will mean all blocks will have bias edges around the perimeter.

From the white solid, cut:
1 strip, 12½" × 42"; crosscut into 1 square, 12½" × 12½"; cut the square in half diagonally to yield 2 large triangles
1 strip, 12" × 42"; crosscut into:
    1 piece, 12" × 17¾"
    1 square, 12" × 12"
1 strip, 7½" × 42"; crosscut into:
    1 square, 7½" × 7½"; cut the square into quarters diagonally to yield 4 medium triangles
    1 piece, 6¼" × 12"

From the gray solid, cut:
3 strips, 12" × 42"; crosscut *1 of the strips* into:
    1 square, 12" × 12"
    1 square, 7½" × 7½"; cut the square into quarters diagonally to yield 4 medium triangles
3 strips, 6¼" × 42"; crosscut *2 of the strips* into:
    1 strip, 6¼" × 29¼"
    1 strip, 6¼" × 17¾"*
6 strips, 2½" × 42"

*Save the leftover second and third strip for the border.

Making the Heart

Use a ¼" seam allowance. Press all seam allowances as indicated by the arrows.

1. Working on a design wall or other large surface, arrange the assorted small triangles in a heart pattern consisting of whole and half Hourglass blocks, following the suggested layout of fabric numbers if desired. The heart should be eight blocks wide and seven blocks tall.

> ### Extra Triangles for Variety
>
> For colors 17–20, you will not use all of the cut triangles, but cutting the same number of triangles from all of the fabrics is faster *and* allows more flexibility to switch colors around during the layout process. ↰

Color placement

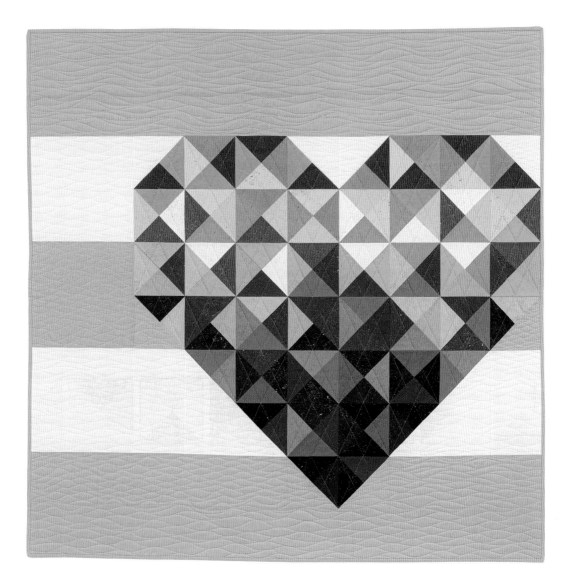

>> Designed by Diane Brinton and Audrey Mann; pieced and quilted by Audrey Mann <<

2. To piece each Hourglass block, sew small triangles together in pairs, joining them along their short edges. Press. Sew the two pairs together. Press. Trim to 6¼" square, including seam allowances. Make 32 Hourglass blocks.

3. To piece each half Hourglass block, sew a pair of small triangles together. Press. Do not trim these blocks yet. Make 12 half blocks.

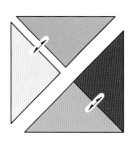 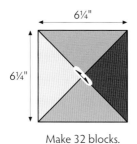

Make 32 blocks.

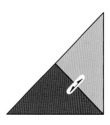

Make 12 half blocks.

4. In row 1, complete the half blocks by adding a white medium-size triangle along the diagonal edge. Press. Trim each block to 6¼" square, including seam allowances. In rows 4 and 7, complete the half blocks by adding a gray medium-size triangle. Trim as before.

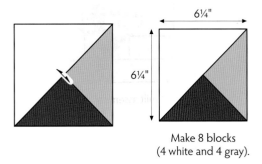

Make 8 blocks
(4 white and 4 gray).

5. Sew the blocks in rows 1 and 2 together by first sewing the blocks into rows and pressing. Then, join the rows. Last, add the white 12" square to the left side. The section should measure 12" × 58", including seam allowances.

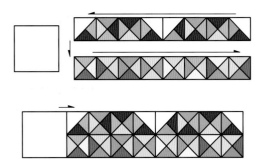

Make rows 1 and 2 section,
12" × 58".

6. Sew the blocks in rows 3 and 4 together by first sewing the blocks into rows and pressing. Then, join the rows. Last, sew the gray 12" square to the left side. The section should measure 12" × 58", including seam allowances.

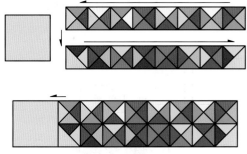

Make rows 3 and 4 section,
12" × 58".

7. In rows 5 and 6, trim the half Hourglass blocks to 6⅝" × 6⅝", as if each were a complete square.

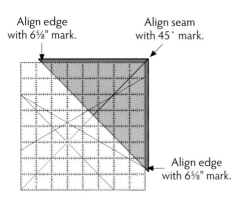

· Piece & Love ·

8. Sew the trimmed half blocks to the adjoining full block on both ends of row 5. Sew a white large triangle to the diagonal edge of the half-square units. Press, then trim to 12" square, including seam allowances.

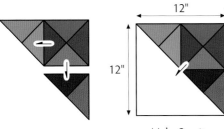

Make 2 units.

9. Sew the remaining four blocks in rows 5 and 6 together by piecing the blocks together in pairs, then sewing the pairs together. Add the pieced triangle units from step 8 to both sides of the center square. Sew the white 12" × 17¾" piece to the left side and the white 6¼" × 12" piece to the right side. The section should be 12" × 58", including seam allowances.

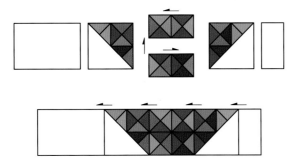

Make rows 5 and 6 section,
12" × 58".

10. Sew the blocks in row 7 together, then sew the gray 6¼" × 29¼" piece to the left side and the gray 6¼" × 17¾" piece to the right side. The section should be 6¼" × 58", including seam allowances.

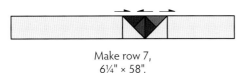

Make row 7,
6¼" × 58".

Assembling the Quilt Top

1. Sew the gray 12" × 42" strips together end to end. Trim the pieced strip to 12" × 58" to make the top row of the quilt.

2. Sew the gray 6¼"-wide strips together end to end. Trim the strip to 6¼" × 58" to make the bottom row of the quilt.

3. Sew all background stripes and heart rows together as shown in the quilt assembly diagram. The quilt top should be 58" square.

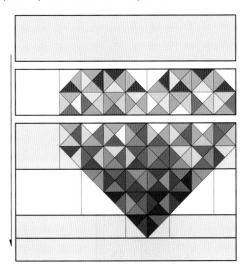

Quilt assembly

Finishing the Quilt

For more details on any finishing steps, visit ShopMartingale.com/HowtoQuilt for free downloadable information.

1. Prepare the quilt backing so it is about 6" larger in both directions than the quilt top.

2. Layer the backing, batting, and quilt top. Baste the layers together.

3. Hand or machine quilt as desired. The quilt shown is quilted with random diagonal lines in the heart and organic waves in the background stripes.

4. Use the gray 2½"-wide strips to make double-fold binding; attach the binding to the quilt. Add a label if desired.

Sprinkles

Celebrate your special day with an enormous cupcake! You don't even have to share. Made of strips, squares, and background pieces, this festive treat is one you can whip up in a jiffy. We used large-scale plaids and stripes to give the cupcake wrapper lots of impact with very little effort. No baking required.

FINISHED QUILT: 45½" × 50½"

Materials

Yardage is based on 42"-wide fabric.

- 1⅜ yards of pink solid for background
- 6" × 8" piece of yellow print for sprinkles and candle flame
- 6" ×6" square of blue print for sprinkles
- ⅛ yard of fuchsia print for sprinkles and candle
- ½ yard of white tone on tone for frosting
- 6" × 6" square of green print for sprinkles
- ½ yard of red print for sprinkles and binding
- ½ yard of green plaid for cupcake wrapper
- ½ yard of blue stripe for cupcake wrapper
- 3 yards of fabric for backing
- 52" × 57" piece of batting
- Template plastic

Cutting

All measurements include ¼" seam allowances. Before cutting, trace the left and right triangle patterns on page 19 onto template plastic and cut them out. Use the templates to cut the pieces from the fabrics indicated. Be sure to transfer the dots to the templates and then to the fabric pieces.

From the pink solid, cut:
2 strips, 16½" × 42"; crosscut into:
    2 pieces, 16½" × 22"
    2 pieces, 10" × 10½"
    2 pieces, 6½" × 10"
    2 pieces, 6" × 8½"
    2 squares, 4½" × 4½"
1 strip, 8" × 42"; crosscut into:
    2 pieces, 8" × 10½"
    2 squares, 4½" × 4½"
    1 piece, 2½" × 4½"
    1 square, 2½" × 2½"
2 left and 2 right triangles

From the yellow print, cut:
5 squares, 2½" × 2½"

From the blue print, cut:
3 squares, 2½" × 2½"

Continued on page 14

Continued from page 13

From the fuchsia print, cut:

1 strip, 2½" × 42"; crosscut into:
    1 strip, 2½" × 10½"
    3 squares, 2½" × 2½"

From the white tone on tone, cut:

1 strip, 4½" × 42"; crosscut into:
    2 squares, 4½" × 4½"
    3 pieces, 2½" × 4½"
4 strips, 2½" × 42"; crosscut into:
    2 strips, 2½" × 18½"
    1 strip, 2½" × 16½"
    2 strips, 2½" × 12½"
    2 strips, 2½" × 10½"
    2 strips, 2½" × 8½"
    4 pieces, 2½" × 6½"
    7 squares, 2½" × 2½"

From the green print, cut:

3 squares, 2½" × 2½"

From the red print, cut:

6 strips, 2½" × 42"; crosscut *1 of the strips* into
    3 squares, 2½" × 2½"

From the green plaid, cut:

4 strips, 2½" × 42"; crosscut into 11 strips,
    2½" × 10½"
2 left and 2 right triangles

From the blue stripe, cut:

1 strip, 10½" × 42"; crosscut into 13 strips,
    2½" × 10½"*

**If the stripe runs crosswise instead of lengthwise, cut
5 strips, 2½" × 42"; crosscut into 13 strips, 2½" × 10½".*

Making the Candle Section

Use a ¼" seam allowance. Press all seam allowances as indicated by the arrows.

1. Draw a diagonal line on the back of the pink 2½" square. Place the marked square right sides together with a yellow 2½" square. Sew together on the diagonal line. Trim ¼" from the seam and press to make a half-square-triangle unit measuring 2½" square, including seam allowances.

Make 1 unit,
2½" × 2½".

2. Sew together the pink 2½" × 4½" piece, half-square-triangle unit from step 1, and fuchsia 2½" × 10½" strip in a vertical row. Add pink 16½" × 22" pieces to the left and right sides of the joined pieces to make the candle section. It should be 16½" × 45½", including seam allowances.

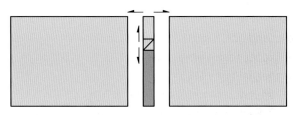

Make 1 candle section,
16½" × 45½".

Making the Frosting Sections

1. Sew a white 2½" square to the left side of a blue 2½" square. Sew another white 2½" square to the top of the blue square.

Make 1 unit.

·Piece & Love·

2. Draw a diagonal line on the wrong side of the step 1 unit. Place the marked unit right sides together with a pink 4½" square. Sew together on the diagonal line. Trim ¼" from the seam and press to make a sprinkle corner unit measuring 4½" square, including seam allowances. Using a yellow 2½" square instead of blue, repeat steps 1 and 2 to make a second sprinkle corner unit.

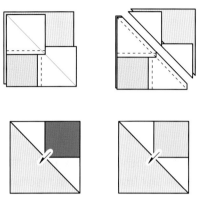

Make 1 blue and 1 yellow unit,
4½" × 4½".

3. Lay out one white 2½" square, two of the assorted print 2½" squares, one white 2½" × 8½" strip, and one white 2½" × 4½" piece in a row. Sew the pieces together to make row 1. In the same manner, join one white 2½" × 6½" piece, one print 2½" square, and one white 2½" × 10½" strip to make row 2. Each row should be 2½" × 18½", including seam allowances. Join the rows.

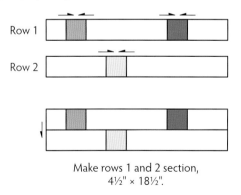

Make rows 1 and 2 section,
4½" × 18½".

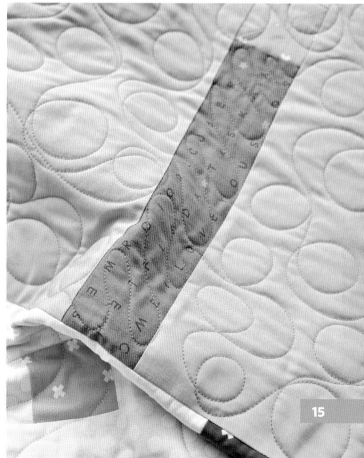

Designed and quilted by Diane Brinton and Audrey Mann; pieced by Diane Brinton

4. Sew together one white 2½" × 18½" strip, one print 2½" square, and one white 2½" × 6½" piece to make row 3. It should be 2½" × 26½", including seam allowances.

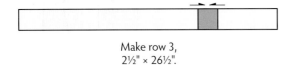

Make row 3,
2½" × 26½".

5. Sew the sprinkle corner units to the left and right ends of joined rows 1 and 2. Sew row 3 to the bottom, then sew pink 6½" × 10" pieces to the left and right sides to make the top frosting section. It should be 6½" × 45½", including seam allowances.

Make 1 top frosting section,
6½" × 45½".

· Piece & Love ·

6. Lay out three assorted print 2½" squares, one white 2½" × 6½" piece, one white 2½" × 4½" piece, and one white 2½" × 10½" strip in a row. Sew the pieces together to make row 4. It should be 2½" × 26½", including seam allowances. In the same manner, join one white 2½" × 4½" piece, two of the assorted print 2½" squares, and one white 2½" × 18½" strip to make row 5. It should be 2½" × 26½", including seam allowances. Join the rows.

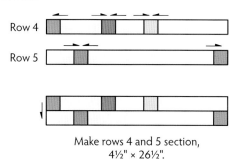

Make rows 4 and 5 section,
4½" × 26½".

7. Lay out one white 2½" square, three assorted print 2½" squares, one white 2½" × 12½" strip, one white 2½" × 6½" piece, and one white 2½" × 8½" strip in a row. Sew the pieces together to make row 6. It should be 2½" × 34½", including seam allowances. In the same manner, join one white 2½" × 12½" strip, two of the assorted print 2½" squares, one white 2½" × 16½" strip, and one white 2½" square to make row 7. It should be 2½" × 34½", including seam allowances. Join the rows.

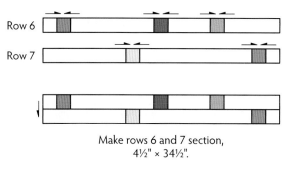

Make rows 6 and 7 section,
4½" × 34½".

8. Draw a diagonal line on the back of a white 4½" square. Place the marked square right sides together with a pink 4½" square. Sew together on the diagonal line. Trim ¼" from the seam and press to

make a half-square-triangle unit measuring 4½" square, including seam allowances. Make two.

Make 2 units,
4½" × 4½".

9. Sew the half-square-triangle units from step 8 to the left and right ends of rows 4 and 5. Sew rows 6 and 7 to the bottom, then add pink 6" × 8½" pieces to the left and right sides to make the bottom frosting section. It should be 8½" × 45½", including seam allowances.

Make 1 bottom frosting section,
8½" × 45½".

Making the Wrapper Sections

1. Matching the marked dots, pin a green plaid left triangle to a pink left triangle. Sew together to make a left-side unit measuring 2½" × 10½", including seam allowances. Repeat to make two left-side units. Using right triangles, make two right-side units.

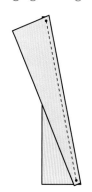 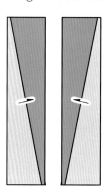

Make 2 of each unit,
2½" × 10½".

2. Referring to the diagram, lay out two pink 8" × 10½" pieces, one left-side unit, seven blue stripe 2½" × 10½" strips, six green plaid 2½" × 10½" strips, and one right-side unit in a row. Sew the pieces together to make the top wrapper section. It should be 10½" × 45½", including seam allowances.

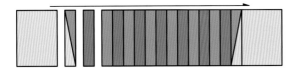

Make 1 top wrapper section,
10½" × 45½".

3. As in the previous step, sew together two pink 10" × 10½" pieces, one left-side unit, six blue stripe 2½" × 10½" strips, five green plaid 2½" × 10½" strips, and one right-side unit in a row to make the bottom wrapper section. It should be 10½" × 45½", including seam allowances.

Make 1 bottom wrapper section,
10½" × 45½".

Assembling the Quilt Top

Sew the candle, frosting, and wrapper sections together to make the quilt top; press well. The quilt top should be 45½" × 50½".

Finishing the Quilt

For more details on any finishing steps, visit ShopMartingale.com/HowtoQuilt for free downloadable information.

1. Prepare the quilt backing so it is about 6" larger in both directions than the quilt top.

2. Layer the backing, batting, and quilt top. Baste the layers together.

3. Hand or machine quilt as desired. The quilt shown is machine quilted with meandering loops in the background, swirls in the frosting, and straight ribbons in the wrapper.

4. Use the red 2½"-wide strips to make double-fold binding; attach the binding to the quilt. Add a label if desired.

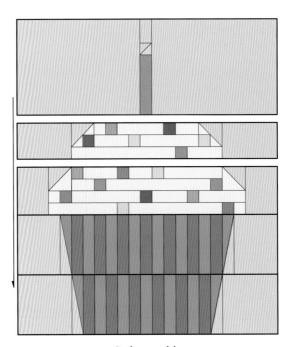

Quilt assembly

Piece & Love

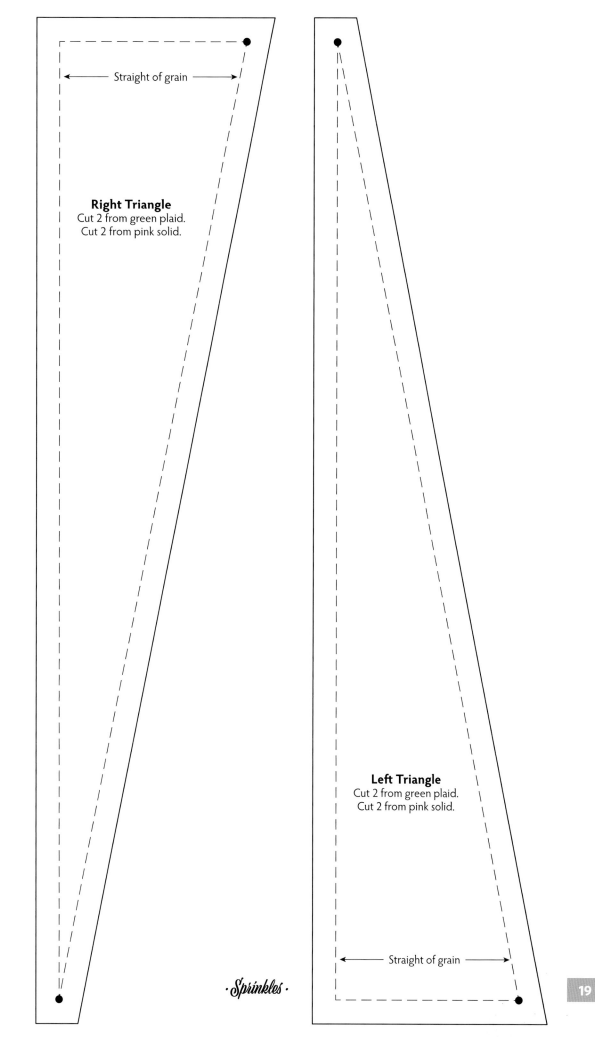

Right Triangle
Cut 2 from green plaid.
Cut 2 from pink solid.

Straight of grain

Left Triangle
Cut 2 from green plaid.
Cut 2 from pink solid.

Straight of grain

·Sprinkles·

Spring Wreath

Spring is in the air with this colorful abstract wreath. Lots of greens with floral accent fabrics mimic springtime blooms. Feel free to mix in some large-scale prints as you create your own Spring Wreath.

FINISHED QUILT: 50½" × 50½" | **FINISHED BLOCK: 5¾" × 5¾"**

Materials

Yardage is based on 42"-wide fabric.

- 6 sets of 4 squares (24 total), 7½" × 7½", OR 6 fat quarters of assorted green prints for wreath fabrics 1, 3, 4, 5, 8, and 10*

- 4 squares, 7½" × 7½", OR 1 fat quarter of dark blue print for wreath fabric 2*

- 3 squares, 7½" × 7½", OR 1 fat quarter of medium blue print for wreath fabric 7*

- 3 squares, 7½" × 7½", OR 1 fat quarter of light pink print for wreath fabric 6*

- 2 squares, 7½" × 7½", OR 1 fat eighth of dark pink print for wreath fabric 11*

- 3 squares, 7½" × 7½", OR 1 fat quarter of yellow print for wreath fabric 9*

- 3 squares, 7½" × 7½", OR 1 fat quarter of green dot for wreath fabric 12*

- 2 squares, 7½" × 7½", OR 1 fat eighth of medium pink print for wreath fabric 13*

- 2 squares, 7½" × 7½", OR 1 fat eighth of light blue print for wreath fabric 14*

*Label fabrics 1–14 as a color progression when laying out the quilt. If you'd like to use a palette similar to that in the featured quilt, refer to the fabric key at right.

- 1⅜ yards of white print for background and border
- ½ yard of green floral for binding
- 3¼ yards of fabric for backing
- 57" × 57" square of batting

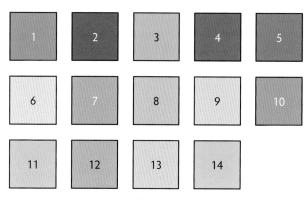

Fabric key

Cutting

All measurements include ¼" seam allowances. If you are using fat quarters and fat eighths for wreath fabrics 1–14, cut them into the number of 7½" squares specified in materials.

From *each* of the assorted print 7½" squares:
Cut each square into quarters diagonally to yield 4 small triangles (184 total; 12 will be extra)

From the green floral, cut:
5 strips, 2½" × 42"

Continued on page 22

Continued from page 21

From the white print, cut:

1 strip, 6¾" × 42"; crosscut into 6 squares,
6¾" × 6¾"; cut the squares in half diagonally
to yield 12 medium triangles

2 strips, 6¼" × 42"; crosscut into:
4 pieces, 6¼" × 12"
4 squares, 6¼" × 6¼"

1 strip, 7½" × 42"; crosscut into 3 squares,
7½" × 7½"; cut the squares into quarters
diagonally to yield 12 small triangles

5 strips, 2½" × 42"

Making the Wreath

Use a ¼" seam allowance. Press all seam allowances
as indicated by the arrows.

1. Working on a design wall or other large surface,
arrange the assorted print small triangles and white
small and medium triangles in a wreath pattern
consisting of whole and half Hourglass blocks,
following the suggested layout of fabric numbers
if desired. The wreath should be eight blocks wide
and eight blocks tall.

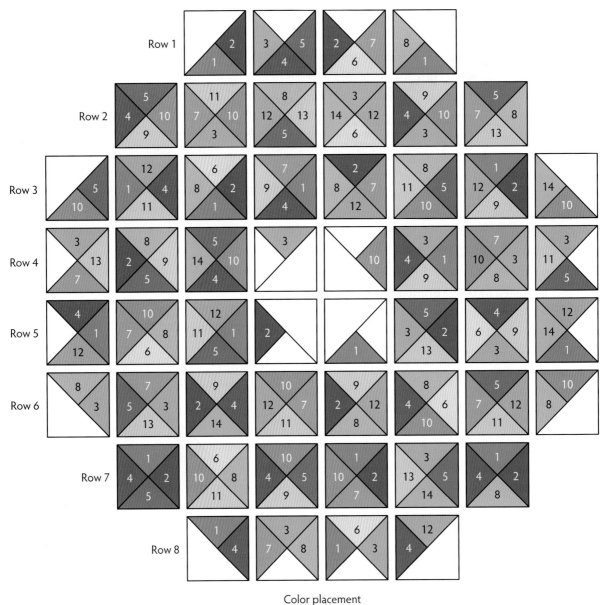

Color placement

Piece & Love

Designed by Diane Brinton and Audrey Mann; pieced and quilted by Diane Brinton

2. To piece each Hourglass block, sew small triangles together in pairs, sewing along the short edges. Press. Sew the two pairs together. Press. Trim to 6¼" square, including seam allowances. Make 40 Hourglass blocks.

3. To piece each half Hourglass block, sew a pair of small triangles together. Press. Do not trim these blocks yet. Make 12.

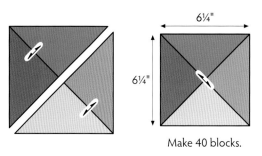

6¼"

6¼"

Make 40 blocks.

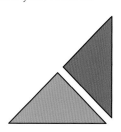
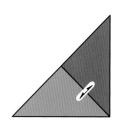

Make 12 half blocks.

4. In rows 1, 3–6, and 8, complete the half blocks by adding a white medium triangle along the diagonal edge. Press. Trim each block to 6¼" square, including seam allowances.

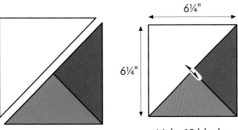

Make 12 blocks.

Assembling the Quilt Top

1. Add the white 6¼" × 12" pieces and 6¼" squares to the quilt layout as shown. Sew the blocks in each row together. Then join the rows. The quilt center should be 46½" square, including seam allowances.

2. Join the white 2½" × 42" strips together end to end. From the pieced strip, cut two long borders, 2½" × 50½", and two short borders, 2½" × 46½".

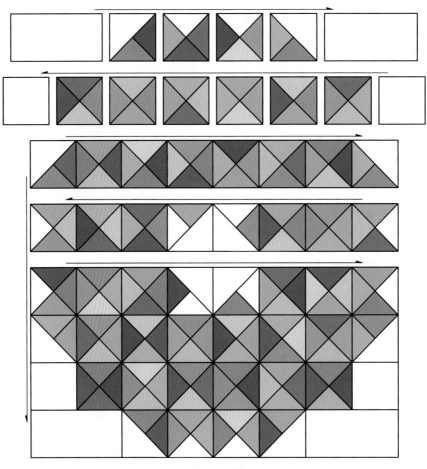

Quilt assembly

·Piece & Love·

3. Sew the 2½" × 46½" borders to the left and right sides of the quilt center. Sew the 2½" × 50½" borders to the top and bottom edges to complete the quilt top. The quilt top should be 50½" square.

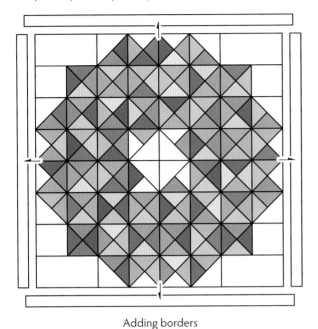

Adding borders

Finishing the Quilt

For more details on any finishing steps, visit ShopMartingale.com/HowtoQuilt for free downloadable information.

1. Prepare the quilt backing so it is about 6" larger in both directions than the quilt top.

2. Layer the backing, batting, and quilt top. Baste the layers together.

3. Hand or machine quilt as desired. The quilt shown is machine quilted with an allover meandering pattern.

4. Use the green floral 2½"-wide strips to make double-fold binding; attach the binding to the quilt. Add a label if desired.

Sundown

Take yourself on a beach vacation with this brilliant sunset beyond the water. The huge stripes of the sky and water go together fast but leave a lasting impression as the backdrop to the pieced and appliquéd sun.

FINISHED QUILT: 70½" × 81"

Materials

Yardage is based on 42"-wide fabric.

- 1⅜ yards of pink stripe for background and binding
- ¾ yard *each* of yellow, orange, red, green, aqua, and blue stripes for background
- ¼ yard *each* of 7 assorted yellow solids for sun
- 4⅞ yards of fabric for backing
- 77" × 87" piece of batting
- 21" × 41" piece of lightweight double-sided fusible web
- 25" length of kitchen string or twine
- Pencil

Cutting

All measurements include ¼" seam allowances.

From the pink stripe, cut:
2 strips, 12" × 42"
8 strips, 2½" × 42"

From *each* of the yellow, orange, red, green, aqua, and blue stripes, cut:
2 strips, 12" × 42" (12 total)

From *each* of the 7 assorted yellow solids, cut:
2 strips, 3⅜" × 42" (14 total); crosscut into
14 squares, 3⅜" × 3⅜" (98 total)

Making the Background Stripes

Use a ¼" seam allowance. Press all seam allowances as indicated by the arrows.

1. Sew the two pink 12" × 42" strips together end to end. Cut the pieced strip into a 70½"-long background piece. Repeat with the remaining stripe fabrics to make seven total background rows.

2. Sew the red and pink background rows together to make the background for the sun. To prevent stretching, pin the pieces together at the ends, midpoint, and quarter points before sewing. The unit should be 23½" × 70½", including seam allowances.

Make 1 background unit,
23½" × 70½".

Designed and pieced by Audrey Mann and Diane Brinton; quilted by Diane Brinton

Making the Sun

1. Lay out the assorted yellow 3⅜" squares in 14 columns of seven squares each; use one square of each yellow in each column. Sew together the squares in each column. Join the columns to make the sun patchwork unit. It should be 20⅝" × 40¾", including seam allowances.

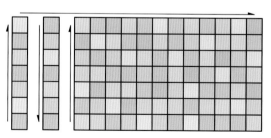

Make 1 sun patchwork unit,
20⅝" × 40¾".

· Piece & Love ·

2. Follow the manufacturer's instructions to apply the fusible web to the back of the sun patchwork. Trim the fusible material to the same size as the patchwork. Tie the string to the pencil and trim the string length to 20". Holding the end of the string at the bottom center seam of the patchwork, draw a half circle on the paper side of the fusible web. Cut through all layers along the drawn line.

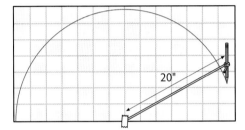

3. Remove the paper backing from the fusible web and place the patchwork sun fusible side down on the right side of the red and pink stripe background unit, matching centers and aligning the bottom edges. Carefully fuse the patchwork sun in place with an iron, following the manufacturer's instructions. Secure the curved edges of the sun with a machine blanket stitch or zigzag stitch. If you don't want the stitching to show, you can use monofilament rather than thread.

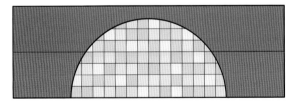

Make 1 sun section, 23½" × 70½".

Assembling the Quilt Top

Sew the yellow and orange stripe rows together and join them to the top of the sun unit. Join the green, aqua, and blue rows and then sew them to the

bottom of the sun to complete the quilt top. To prevent stretching, pin the strips together at the ends, midpoint, and quarter points before sewing. Press well. The quilt top should be 70½" × 81".

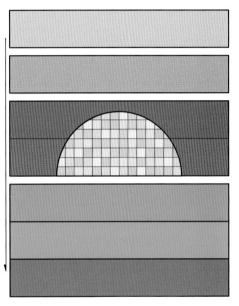

Quilt assembly

Finishing the Quilt

For more details on any finishing steps, visit ShopMartingale.com/HowtoQuilt for free downloadable information.

1. Prepare the quilt backing so it is about 6" larger in both directions than the quilt top.

2. Layer the backing, batting, and quilt top. Baste the layers together.

3. Hand or machine quilt as desired. The quilt shown is machine quilted with horizontal straight and wavy lines in the background and concentric arcs in the sun.

4. Use the pink 2½"-wide strips to make double-fold binding; attach it to the quilt. Add a label if desired.

In Bloom

Bring the sunshine inside with a gigantic blooming sunflower. You can almost smell the summer breeze wafting from the fields. Switch up the colors to represent almost any kind of flower.

FINISHED QUILT: 35½" × 45½"   FINISHED BLOCK: 4½" × 4½"

Materials

Yardage is based on 42"-wide fabric.

- ¼ yard *each* of 1 gold print and 1 gold solid for sunflower
- 10" × 10" square *each* of pink and dark pink prints for sunflower
- 1 fat eighth (9" x 21") *each* of light blue, blue, navy, and purple prints for flower center fabrics 1–4
- 1⅓ yards of sage green solid for background
- ⅛ yard of dark green print for stem and leaf shadows
- ¼ yard of bright green print for stem and leaves
- ½ yard of navy print for binding
- 1½ yards of fabric for backing
- 42" × 52" piece of batting

Cutting

All measurements include ¼" seam allowances.

From *each* of the gold print and gold solid, cut:
1 strip, 3¼" × 42"; crosscut into 10 squares, 3¼" × 3¼" (20 total). Cut *4 of the squares* in half diagonally to yield 8 small triangles (16 total).
1 strip, 2¾" × 42"; crosscut into 4 squares, 2¾" × 2¾" (8 total)

From *each* of the pink and dark pink 10" squares, cut:
6 squares, 3¼" × 3¼" (12 total); cut *2 of the squares* in half diagonally to yield 4 small triangles (8 total)

From the sage green solid, cut:
1 strip, 7⅞" × 42"; crosscut into 2 pieces, 7⅞" × 18½"
2 strips, 6¾" × 42"; crosscut into:
    2 strips, 6¾" × 23"
    4 squares, 5⅜" × 5⅜"; cut each square in half
        diagonally to yield 8 large triangles
2 strips, 5" × 42"; crosscut into:
    1 strip, 5" × 35½"
    4 squares, 5" × 5"
1 strip, 3⅞" × 42"; crosscut into:
    6 squares, 3⅞" × 3⅞"
    3 squares, 3¼" × 3¼"
3 strips, 2¾" × 42"; crosscut into:
    2 strips, 2¾" × 9½"
    6 strips, 2¾" × 7¼"
    3 pieces, 2¾" × 5"
    4 squares, 2¾" × 2¾"

From the dark green print, cut:
1 strip, 3¼" × 42"; crosscut into:
    3 squares, 3¼" × 3¼"
    1 piece, 2¾" × 5"

From *each* of the light blue and blue prints, cut:
2 squares, 6¼" × 6¼" (4 total); cut each square into quarters diagonally to yield 8 medium triangles (16 total; 2 triangles of each color will be extra)

From *each* of the navy and purple prints, cut:
2 squares, 6¼" × 6¼" (4 total); cut each square into quarters diagonally to yield 8 medium triangles (16 total)

Continued on page 32

Designed by Diane Brinton and Audrey Mann; pieced by Audrey Mann; quilted by Diane Brinton

Continued from page 31

From the bright green print, cut:
1 strip, 5" × 42"; crosscut into 4 pieces, 5" × 9½"
1 strip, 2¾" × 42"; crosscut into 2 strips, 2¾" × 9½"

From the navy print for binding, cut:
5 strips, 2½" × 42"

Making the Sunflower Units

Use a ¼" seam allowance. Press all seam allowances as indicated by the arrows.

1. Draw a diagonal line on the wrong side of the gold solid 3¼" squares and dark pink 3¼" squares.

2. With right sides together, layer a marked gold square on a gold print square. Sew together ¼" on either side of the drawn line. Cut on the line to make two half-square-triangle units. Trim each unit to 2¾" square, including seam allowances. Make eight gold half-square-triangle units.

Make 8 units.

Piece & Love

3. Using the remaining two marked gold solid squares and two pink 3¼" squares, repeat step 2 to make four gold/pink half-square-triangle units. In the same manner, use two marked dark pink squares and two pink 3¼" squares to make four dark pink/pink half-square-triangle units. Use the remaining two marked dark pink squares and two gold print 3¼" squares to make four dark pink/gold units. Trim each unit to 2¾" square, including seam allowances.

Make 4 units, 2¾" × 2¾". Make 4 units, 2¾" × 2¾". Make 4 units, 2¾" × 2¾".

4. Draw a diagonal line on the wrong side of the gold solid and gold print 2¾" squares.

5. With right sides together, place a marked gold solid square on the left end of a sage green 2¾" × 5" piece. Sew on the diagonal line. Trim ¼" beyond the seam and press the resulting triangle open. Using a marked gold print square, repeat on the other end of the sage green piece, making sure to mirror image the diagonal to create the point in the center. Make three sage green flying-geese units measuring 2¾" × 5", including seam allowances.

 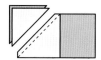

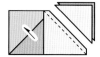

Make 3 units, 2¾" × 5".

6. Using a dark green 2¾" × 5" piece, repeat step 5 to make a dark green flying-geese unit.

Make 1 unit, 2¾" × 5".

7. Sew a gold solid and gold print small triangle to a gold half-square triangle as shown, matching the gold print to the gold solid for contrast. Make eight units.

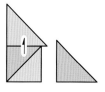

Make 8 units.

8. Using a pink/dark pink half-square-triangle unit and pink and dark pink small triangles, repeat step 7 to make a pink pieced triangle. Make four units.

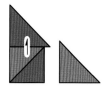

Make 4 units.

9. Sew a sage green large triangle to the diagonal edge of a gold pieced triangle to make a corner petal unit. Trim the unit to 5" square, including seam allowances. Make eight units.

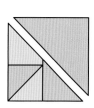 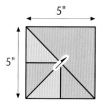

5"
5"

Make 8 units.

10. Join one each of gold/pink and dark pink/gold half-square-triangle units. Add a sage green or dark green flying-geese unit to the top edge to make a middle petal unit. The unit should be 5" square, including seam allowances. Make four units.

Make 4 units, 5" × 5".

Assembling the Sunflower Section

1. Arrange the assorted light blue, blue, navy, and purple triangles in an octagon shape consisting of whole and half Hourglass blocks. The octagon should be three blocks wide and three blocks tall.

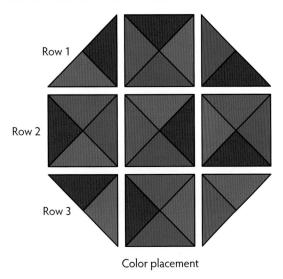

Color placement

2. To piece each Hourglass block, sew small triangles together in pairs along their short edges. Press. Sew the two pairs together. Press. Trim to 5" square, including seam allowances. Make five Hourglass blocks.

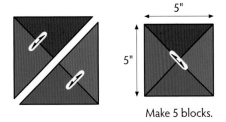

Make 5 blocks.

3. To piece each half Hourglass block, sew a pair of small triangles together. Press. Do not trim these blocks yet. Make four.

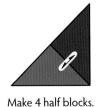

Make 4 half blocks.

4. In rows 1 and 3, complete the half blocks by adding a pink pieced triangle along the diagonal edge. Press seam allowances open. Trim each block to 5" square, including seam allowances. Make four.

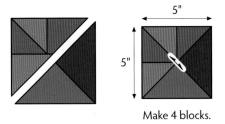

Make 4 blocks.

5. Lay out four sage green 5" squares, eight corner petal units, four middle petal units, the blocks from step 4, and the Hourglass blocks in five rows as shown. Sew together the pieces in each row. Join the rows to make a sunflower unit measuring 23" square, including seam allowances.

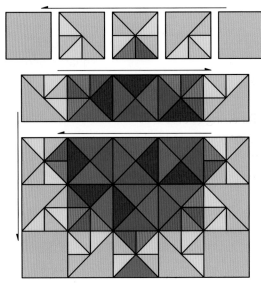

Make 1 sunflower unit, 23" × 23".

Reduce Bulk

Be sure to trim off any triangle points that extend past the edge of each block. This will help reduce seam bulk. ←

· Piece & Love ·

6. Sew the sage green 6¾" × 23" strips to the left and right sides of the sunflower unit. Make sure the dark green flying-geese unit is on the bottom. The sunflower section should be 23" × 35½", including seam allowances.

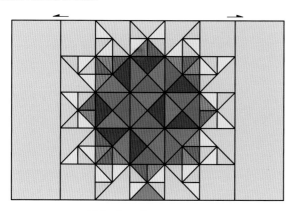

Make 1 sunflower section,
23" × 35½".

Making the Stem

1. Draw a diagonal line on the wrong side of the sage green 3¼" squares, 3⅞" squares, and 2¾" squares.

2. Referring to step 2 of "Making the Sunflower Units," page 32, use marked sage green 3¼" squares and the dark green 3¼" squares to make six half-square-triangle units.

3. Position a marked sage green 3⅞" square right sides together in the lower-left and upper-right corners of a bright green 5" × 9½" piece. Sew the squares to the piece along the drawn diagonal lines. Trim the corners ¼" from the seams and press to make leaf unit A.

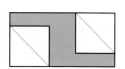 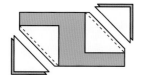

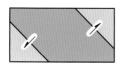

Make 1 leaf unit A,
5" × 9½".

4. Positioning the marked squares in the upper-left and lower-right corners instead, repeat step 3 to make a reversed leaf unit A.

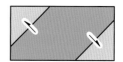

Make 1 reversed leaf unit A,
5" × 9½".

5. Lay out two half-square-triangle units, two sage green 2¾" × 7¼" strips, and the leaf unit A in three rows. Sew together the pieces in each row. Join the rows to make a leaf block A. In the same manner, use the reversed leaf unit A to make a reversed leaf block A. The blocks should be 9½" square, including seam allowances.

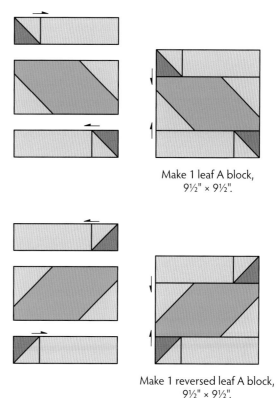

Make 1 leaf A block,
9½" × 9½".

Make 1 reversed leaf A block,
9½" × 9½".

6. Place marked 3⅞" and 2¾" squares right sides together on opposite corners of the bright green 5" × 9½" piece as shown. Sew on the diagonal lines. Trim the corners ¼" from the seams and press the resulting triangles open. Place a second marked

2¾" square on the same end as the first 2¾" square. Sew on the diagonal line and trim as before to make a leaf unit B.

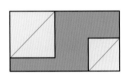

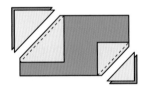

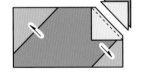

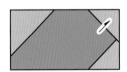

Make 1 leaf unit B,
5" × 9½".

7. Positioning the marked squares in the mirror-image corners, repeat step 6 to make a reversed leaf unit B.

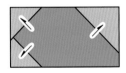

Make 1 reversed leaf unit B,
5" × 9½".

8. Sew together a half-square-triangle unit and a sage green 2¾" × 7¼" strip. Add a sage green 2¾" × 9½" strip and the leaf unit B to the row to make a leaf block B. In the same manner, use the reversed leaf unit B to make a reversed leaf block B. The blocks should be 9½" square, including seam allowances.

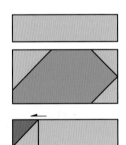

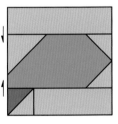

Make 1 leaf B block,
9½" × 9½".

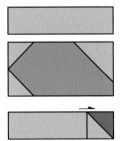

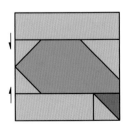

Make 1 reversed leaf B block,
9½" × 9½".

· Piece & Love ·

9. Referring to the diagram, lay out the leaf blocks and bright green 2¾" × 9½" strips in two rows. Sew together the pieces in each row. Join the rows to make the stem unit. It should be 18½" × 20¾", including seam allowances.

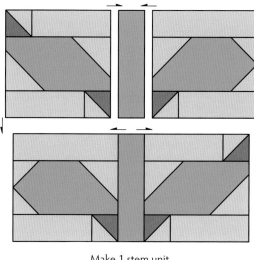

Make 1 stem unit,
18½" × 20¾".

10. Sew sage green 7⅞" × 18½" pieces to the sides of the stem unit to make the stem section. It should be 18½" × 35½", including seam allowances.

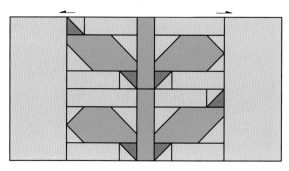

Make 1 stem section,
18½" × 35½".

Assembling the Quilt Top

Sew the sage green 5" × 35½" strip, sunflower section, and stem section together and press. The quilt top should be 35½" × 45½".

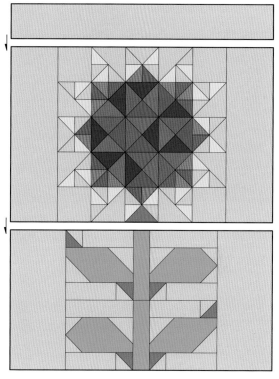

Quilt assembly

Finishing the Quilt

For more details on any finishing steps, visit ShopMartingale.com/HowtoQuilt for free downloadable information.

1. Prepare the quilt backing so it is about 6" larger in both directions than the quilt top.

2. Layer the backing, batting, and quilt top. Baste the layers together.

3. Hand or machine quilt as desired. The quilt shown is machine quilted with an allover floral pattern.

4. Use the navy 2½"-wide strips to make double-fold binding; attach the binding to the quilt. Add a label if desired.

Sweet Strawberry

Remember summers past with sweet, ripe strawberries warmed by the sun and eaten in the field. This larger-than-life, luscious berry made from quarter-square triangles in a variety of pinks and reds could even be chocolate-dipped for your valentine.

FINISHED QUILT: 41" × 50½" | **FINISHED BLOCK: 5¾" × 5¾"**

Materials

Yardage is based on 42"-wide fabric. Fat eighths are 9" x 21".

- 4 fat eighths of assorted green prints and solids for stem fabrics A–D
- 4 fat eighths of assorted red prints and solids for strawberry fabrics 1, 2, 11, and 13
- 6 fat eighths of assorted pink prints and solids for strawberry fabrics 3, 4, 5, 6, 8, and 9
- 3 fat eighths of assorted fuchsia prints and solids for strawberry fabrics 7, 10, and 12
- 1⅛ yards of light blue solid for background
- ⅛ yard of black print for seeds
- ½ yard of pink solid for binding
- 2⅝ yards of fabric for backing
- 47" × 57" piece of batting

*Label green fabrics A–D and pink fabrics 1–14 as a color progression when laying out the quilt. If you'd like to use a palette similar to that in the featured quilt, refer to the fabric key, below.

Cutting

All measurements include ¼" seam allowances.

From *each* of the assorted green prints and solids, cut:
1 square, 7½" × 7½"; cut into quarters diagonally to yield 4 small triangles (16 total)

From *each* of the assorted red, pink, and fuchsia prints and solids, cut:
2 squares, 7½" × 7½"; cut into quarters diagonally to yield 8 small triangles of each fabric (104 total)

From the light blue solid, cut:
1 strip, 12½" × 42"; crosscut into:
    1 square, 12½" × 12½"; cut the square in half diagonally to yield 2 large triangles
    4 squares, 6¾" × 6¾"; cut the squares in half diagonally to yield 8 medium triangles
1 strip, 12" × 42"; crosscut into 4 pieces, 9¼" × 12"
1 strip, 7" × 42"; crosscut into:
    2 squares, 6¼" × 6¼"
    2 strips, 3½" × 23½"
2 strips, 2½" × 41"

Continued on page 40

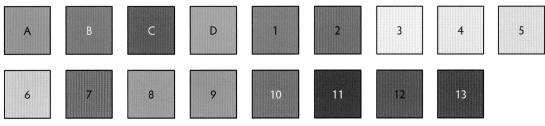

Fabric key

Continued from page 39

From the black print, cut:

1 strip, 2" × 42"; crosscut into 14 squares, 2" × 2"

From the pink solid for binding, cut:

5 strips, 2½" × 42"

Making the Strawberry

Use a ¼" seam allowance. Press all seam allowances as indicated by the arrows.

1. Working on a design wall or other large surface, arrange the assorted print small triangles in a strawberry pattern consisting of whole and half Hourglass blocks, following the suggested layout of fabric numbers if desired. The strawberry should be six blocks wide and eight blocks tall.

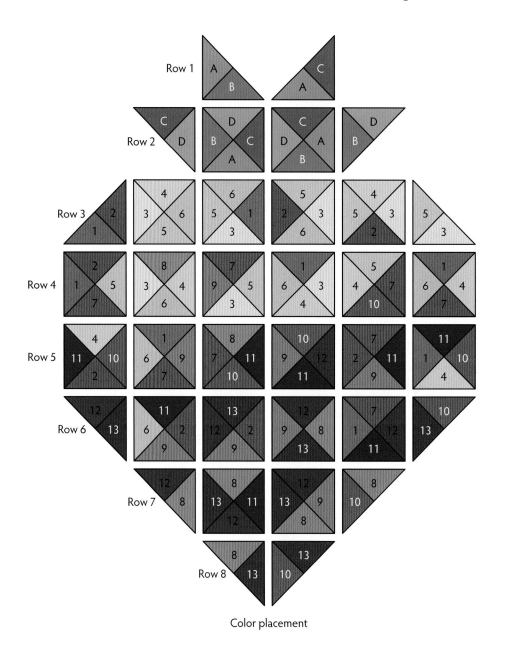

Color placement

2. To piece each Hourglass block, sew small triangles together in pairs along their short edges. Press. Sew the two pairs together. Press. Trim to 6¼" square, including seam allowances. Make two green Hourglass blocks and 22 pink/red Hourglass blocks.

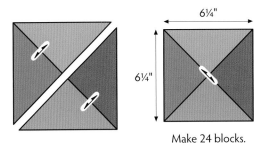

6¼"

6¼"

Make 24 blocks.

3. To piece each half Hourglass block, sew a pair of small triangles together. Press. Make four green half blocks and eight pink/red half blocks. Do not trim these blocks yet.

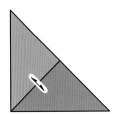

Make 12 half blocks.

4. In rows 1, 2, 3, and 6, complete the half blocks by adding a light blue medium triangle along the diagonal edge. Press. Trim each block to 6¼" square, including seam allowances.

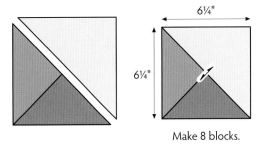

6¼"

6¼"

Make 8 blocks.

5. Sew together two light blue 6¼" squares and two half-green blocks in row 1. Then join two half-green blocks and two Hourglass blocks in row 2. Join the rows and add light blue 9¼" × 12" pieces to the left and right ends to make the stem section. It should measure 12" × 41", including seam allowances.

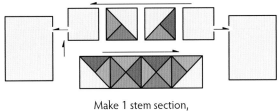

Make 1 stem section,
12" × 41".

Designed by Diane Brinton and Audrey Mann; pieced and quilted by Diane Brinton

· Piece & Love ·

6. In rows 7 and 8, trim the pink/red half Hourglass blocks to 6⅝" × 6⅝", as if each were a complete square.

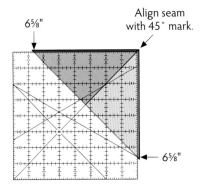

7. Mark a diagonal line on the back of each black 2" square. Refer to the quilt assembly diagram on page 44 for placement of the "seeds" in the whole and half Hourglass blocks in rows 3–8. Place a marked black square on the corner of one of the blocks or half blocks. Sew on the diagonal line and trim the excess corner ¼" from the seam. Press. Repeat with all blocks indicated in the quilt assembly diagram.

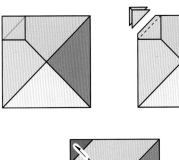

8. Sew the blocks in rows 3–6 together. Join the rows. Sew light blue 3½" × 23½" strips to the left and right sides to make the strawberry top section. It should be 23½" × 41", including seam allowances.

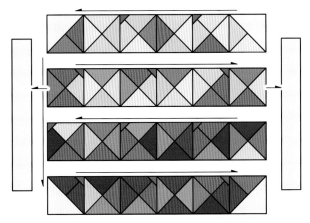

Make 1 strawberry top section, 23½" × 41".

9. Sew the trimmed half blocks from step 6 to the adjoining full block on both ends of row 7. Sew a light blue large triangle to the diagonal edge of the half-square units. Trim to 12" square, including seam allowances.

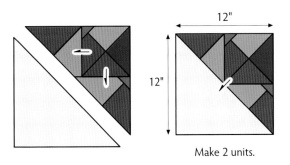

Make 2 units.

10. Sew the left and right pieced triangle units together, then sew the remaining light blue 9¼" × 12" pieces to the left and right sides to make the strawberry bottom section. It should be 12" × 41", including seam allowances.

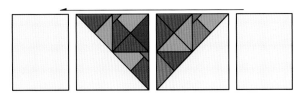

Make 1 strawberry bottom section, 12" × 41".

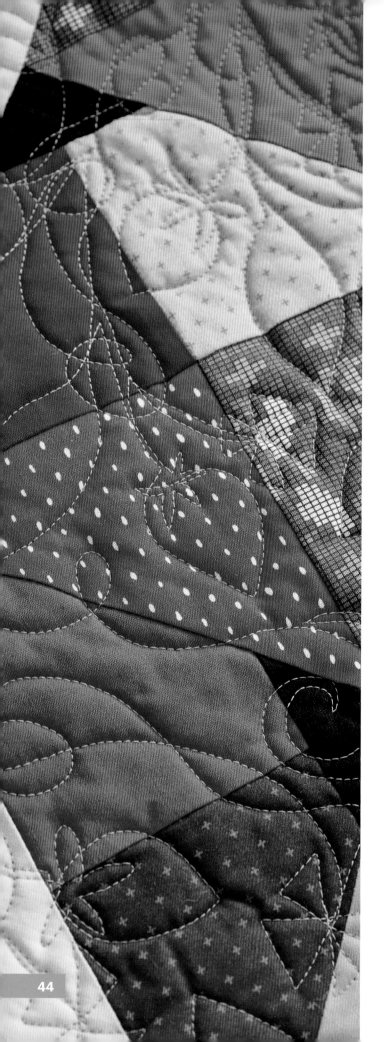

Assembling the Quilt Top

Sew the light blue 2½" × 41" border strips, stem section, and strawberry sections together, matching seams where possible. The quilt top should be 41" × 50½".

Quilt assembly

Finishing the Quilt

For more details on any finishing steps, visit ShopMartingale.com/HowtoQuilt for free downloadable information.

1. Prepare the quilt backing so it is about 6" larger in both directions than the quilt top.

2. Layer the backing, batting, and quilt top. Baste the layers together.

3. Hand or machine quilt as desired. The quilt shown is machine quilted with an allover pattern of strawberries and leaves.

4. Use the pink 2½"-wide strips to make double-fold binding; attach the binding to the quilt. Add a label if desired.

Nordic Frost

Celebrate the northern climes with an icy throw inspired by knitted sweaters and snowflakes. Striped borders add a wool-blanket vibe, anchoring the central snowflake motif. Nordic Frost is perfect for a cozy read by the fire or bundling up to watch the snow fall.

FINISHED QUILT: 64½" × 80½"

Materials

Yardage is based on 42"-wide fabric.

- 1⅓ yards of navy print (fabric A) for blocks, stripe borders, and binding
- ⅝ yard of dark blue print (fabric B) for blocks and stripe borders
- ½ yard of medium blue print (fabric C) for blocks and stripe borders
- ⅓ yard of light blue print (fabric D) for blocks and stripe borders
- 4⅔ yards of white solid (fabric E) for background
- 5 yards of fabric for backing
- 73" × 89" piece of batting

Fabric key

Cutting

All measurements include ¼" seam allowances.

From the navy print (A), cut:
4 strips, 4½" × 42"
9 strips, 2½" × 42"; crosscut *2 of the strips* into:
    2 pieces, 2½" × 4½"
    24 squares, 2½" × 2½"
    4 pieces, 1½" × 2½"
    4 squares, 1½" × 1½"

From the dark blue print (B), cut:
6 strips, 2½" × 42"; crosscut *2 of the strips* into:
    4 pieces, 2½" × 4½"
    20 squares, 2½" × 2½
1 strip, 2" × 42"; crosscut into:
    4 squares, 2" × 2"
    2 pieces, 1½" × 2½"

From the medium blue print (C), cut:
2 strips, 2½" × 42; crosscut into:
    2 pieces, 2½" × 4½"
    28 squares, 2½" × 2½"
4 strips, 2" × 42"
1 strip, 1½" × 42"; crosscut into 2 pieces, 1½" × 2½"

From the light blue print (D), cut:
4 strips, 1½" × 42"
1 strip, 2½" × 42"; crosscut into 8 squares, 2½" × 2½"

Continued on page 47

Continued from page 45

From the white solid (E), cut:

3 strips, 10½" × 42"

4 strips, 6½" × 42"; crosscut into:

    4 pieces, 6½" × 18½"

    4 pieces, 6½" × 12½"

4 strips, 5" × 42"

3 strips, 4½" × 42"; crosscut into:

    8 squares, 4½" × 4½"

    24 pieces, 2½" × 4½"

    12 pieces, 1½" × 4½"

1 strip, 3" × 42"; crosscut into:

    4 pieces, 3" × 3½"

    4 pieces, 2" × 3"

17 strips, 2½" × 42"; crosscut *10 of the strips* into:

    8 pieces, 2½" × 10½"

    8 pieces, 2½" × 8½"

    84 squares, 2½" × 2½"

9 strips, 1½" × 42"; crosscut *5 of the strips* into:

    8 pieces, 1½" × 5½"

    12 pieces, 1½" × 2½"

    4 pieces, 1½" × 2"

    56 squares, 1½" × 1½"

Making the Half-Square-Triangle Units

Use a ¼" seam allowance. Press all seam allowances as indicated by the arrows.

1. Draw a diagonal line on the back of 56 E 2½" squares and four C 2½" squares.

2. Place a marked E 2½" square right sides together with an A 2½" square. Sew together on the diagonal line. Trim ¼" from the seam and press to make an A/E half-square-triangle unit measuring 2½" × 2½", including seam allowances. Make 12.

Make 12 A/E units,
2½" × 2½".

3. Using the color combinations shown, repeat step 2 to make 32 additional half-square-triangle units. (Set aside the remaining marked E 2½" squares for the next section.)

Make 8 B/E units,
2½" × 2½".

Make 12 C/E units,
2½" × 2½".

Make 8 D/E units,
2½" × 2½".

Make 4 A/C units,
2½" × 2½".

Making the Flying-Geese Units

1. Draw a diagonal line on the back of four A, eight B, and four C 2½" squares. Also mark 56 E 1½" squares.

2. With right sides together, place a marked E 2½" square on the left end of an A 2½" × 4½" piece. Sew on the diagonal line. Trim ¼" beyond the seam and press the resulting triangle open. Using a second marked square, repeat on the other end of the A piece, making sure to mirror image the diagonal to create the point in the center. Make two large E/A flying-geese units measuring 2½" × 4½", including seam allowances.

Make 2 E/A units,
2½" × 4½".

3. Using the pieces indicated in the diagram, repeat step 2 to make 14 additional large flying-geese units.

Make 2 A/E units,
2½" × 4½".

Make 4 E/B units,
2½" × 4½".

Make 4 B/E units,
2½" × 4½".

Make 2 E/C units,
2½" × 4½".

Make 2 C/E units,
2½" × 4½".

4. Using marked E 1½" squares and an A 1½" × 2½" piece, repeat step 2 to make a small E/A flying-geese unit measuring 1½" × 2½", including seam allowances. Make four. Using the pieces indicated in the diagram, make four additional small flying-geese units.

Make 4 E/A units,
1½" × 2½".

Make 2 E/B units,
1½" × 2½".

Make 2 E/C units,
1½" × 2½".

5. Position a marked E 1½" square in a remaining corner of a small E/A flying-geese unit. Stitch, trim, and press as before. Repeat at the other end of the flying-geese unit to make a double flying-geese unit. Make four. (Set aside remaining marked E 1½" squares for the next section.)

Make 4 E/A units,
1½" × 2½".

Making the Square-in-a-Square Units

1. Place marked E 1½" squares in opposite corners of an A 2½" square, right sides together. Sew on the diagonal lines; trim ¼" from the seams. Press the triangles open. Repeat in the remaining corners to make an A square-in-a-square unit measuring 2½" square, including seam allowances. Make four units.

Make 4 A units,
2½" × 2½".

2. Using a C 2½" square instead of A, repeat step 1 to make four C square-in-a-square units.

Make 4 C units,
2½" × 2½".

Making the Star Block

Lay out four E 2½" squares, four C/E half-square-triangle units, four A/E half-square-triangle units, and four A/C half-square-triangle units as shown. Join the pieces in each row. Join the rows to make a Star block, 8½" square, including seam allowances.

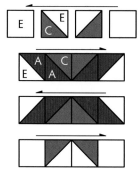
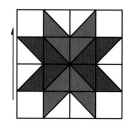
Make 1 Star block,
8½" × 8½".

⇛ ➡ *Designed, pieced, and quilted by Audrey Mann and Diane Brinton* ⬅ ⇚

Making the Corner Blocks

1. Sew together an A 1½" square and an E 1½" × 2" piece in a vertical row. Sew an E 3" × 3½" piece to the right edge of the vertical row. Sew together an E 2" × 3" piece and a B 2" square in a horizontal row; add this to the bottom of the other pieces. Make four units measuring 4½" square, including seam allowances.

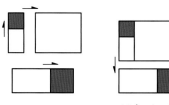

Make 4 units,
4½" × 4½".

2. Sew together an A/E half-square-triangle unit and an E 2½" square in a horizontal row. Add an E 2½" × 4½" piece to the bottom edge. Make four. Repeat with the same pieces to make four mirror-image units measuring 4½" square, including seam allowances.

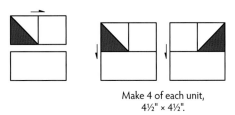

Make 4 of each unit,
4½" × 4½".

3. Sew together one E 2½" square, two B/E half-square-triangle units, and one B 2½" square in pairs as shown. Join the pairs. Make four units measuring 4½" square, including seam allowances.

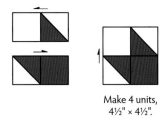

Make 4 units,
4½" × 4½".

4. Using C pieces instead of B, repeat step 3 to make four units.

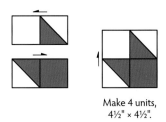

Make 4 units,
4½" × 4½".

5. Sew together an E 2½" square and a D/E half-square-triangle unit in a vertical row. Add an E 2½" × 4½" piece to the right edge. Make four units measuring 4½" square, including seam allowances. Repeat with the same pieces to make four mirror-image units.

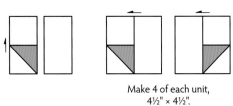

Make 4 of each unit,
4½" × 4½".

6. Lay out one piece each from steps 1–5 and two E 4½" squares in three rows. Sew together the pieces in each row. Join the rows to make a corner block. Make four corner blocks measuring 12½" square, including seam allowances.

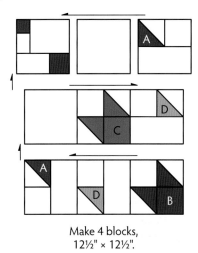

Make 4 blocks,
12½" × 12½".

7. Sew an E 6½" × 12½" piece to the left edge of a corner block. Add an E 6½" × 18½" piece to the top edge to make a corner unit. Make four units measuring 18½" square, including seam allowances.

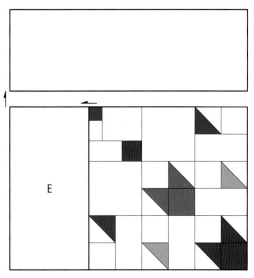

Make 4 corner units,
18½" × 18½".

Making the Middle Edge Blocks

1. Sew together an A Square-in-a-Square unit, E 1½" × 2½" piece, and C Square-in-a-Square unit in a vertical row. Sew E 1½" × 5½" pieces to the side edges. Make four units measuring 4½" × 5½", including seam allowances.

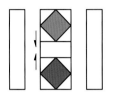

Make 4 units,
4½" × 5½".

2. Join one E/C small flying-geese unit, two E 1½" × 2½" pieces, and one double flying-geese unit in a vertical row. Add E 1½" × 4½" pieces to either side of the row. Make two units measuring 4½" square, including seam allowances. Make two additional units using E/B small flying-geese units instead of E/C.

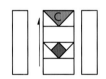

Make 2 vertical units,
4½" × 4½".

Make 2 horizontal units,
4½" × 4½".

3. Referring to the top half of the diagram above right, join a unit from step 1, an E 1½" × 4½" piece, and a vertical unit from step 2 in a row. Add E 2½" × 10½" strips to the side edges of the joined pieces to make a vertical middle edge block. Make two blocks measuring 8½" × 10½", including seam allowances. Using horizontal pieces from step 2

instead, make two horizontal middle edge blocks; be sure to rotate the unit from step 1 as shown.

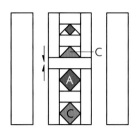 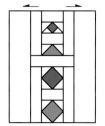

Make 2 vertical
Middle Edge blocks,
8½" × 10½".

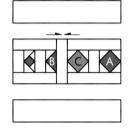 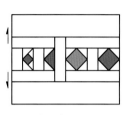

Make 2 horizontal
Middle Edge blocks,
8½" × 10½".

Making the Arrow Blocks

Sew together one each of E/A, A/E, E/B, and B/E large flying-geese units in a column. Add an E 2½" × 8½" strip to either side of the joined flying geese to make a vertical Arrow block. Make two. Using B/E, E/B, C/E, and E/C flying-geese units, make two horizontal Arrow blocks. The blocks should be 8½" square, including seam allowances.

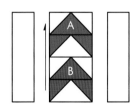 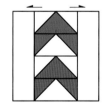

Make 2 vertical Arrow blocks,
8½" × 8½".

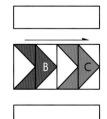 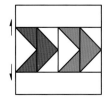

Make 2 horizontal Arrow blocks,
8½" × 8½".

Assembling the Quilt Center

1. Referring to the quilt assembly diagram below, lay out four corner units and the Star block in three rows. Fill in the vertical areas between the corner units with vertical middle edge blocks and vertical Arrow blocks. Fill in the horizontal areas between the corner units with horizontal middle edge blocks and horizontal Arrow blocks.

2. Sew together the middle edge and Arrow blocks. Then sew together the units and blocks in each row. Join the rows to make the quilt center, which should be 44½" square, including seam allowances.

Quilt assembly

Assembling the Quilt Top

1. Join three E 10½" × 42" strips end to end, then cut into two side borders, 10½" × 44½". Sew to the left and right sides of the quilt top.

2. Join four A 4½" × 42" strips end to end, then cut into two borders, 4½" × 64½".

3. Join four B 2½" × 42" strips end to end, then cut into two borders, 2½" × 64½".

4. Join four C 2" strips end to end, then cut into two borders, 2" × 64½".

· Piece & Love ·

5. Join four D 1½" strips end to end, then cut into two borders, 1½" × 64½".

6. Join four E 5" strips end to end, then cut into two borders, 5" × 64½".

7. Join seven E 2½" strips end to end, then cut into four borders, 2½" × 64½".

8. Join four E 1½" strips end to end, then cut into two borders, 1½" × 64½".

9. Referring to the top of quilt assembly diagram below, lay out the 64½"-long strips in order: 5" E, D, 2½" E, B, 1½" E, A, 2½" E, and C. Pin the strips together to prevent stretching. Sew the strips together and press. Make two.

10. Sew the stripe sections to the top and bottom edges with the C strips adjoining the quilt top to complete the quilt top. The quilt top should be 64½" × 80½".

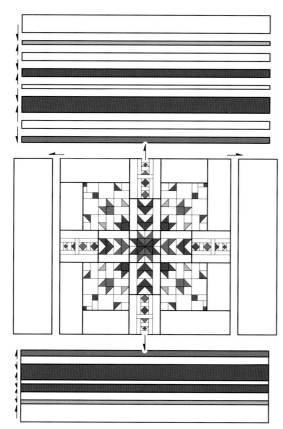

Adding borders

Finishing the Quilt

For more details on any finishing steps, visit ShopMartingale.com/HowtoQuilt for free downloadable information.

1. Prepare the quilt backing so it is about 8" larger in both directions than the quilt top.

2. Layer the backing, batting, and quilt top. Baste the layers together.

3. Hand or machine quilt as desired. The quilt shown is machine quilted with an allover pattern of bare winter branches.

4. Use the navy 2½"-wide strips to make double-fold binding; attach the binding to the quilt. Add a label if desired.

Piece & Light

Spend some time stargazing with this faceted Sawtooth Star. Bright colors really shine against the night sky. Choose your own palette of 16 colors to make your quilt the star of the show.

FINISHED QUILT: 50½" × 58" | **FINISHED BLOCK: 5¾" × 5¾"**

Materials

Yardage is based on 42"-wide fabric. Fat eighths are 9" × 21".

- 16 fat eighths of assorted light, medium, and dark prints for star; sort fabrics into colors 1–16*
- 2⅓ yards of navy solid for background and binding
- 3¼ yards of fabric for backing
- 57" × 64" piece of batting

*Label your fabrics as a color progression when laying out the quilt. We used mostly warm colors (red, pink, orange, and yellow) for fabrics 1–8 and mostly cool colors (blue and green) for fabrics 9–16. If you'd like to use a palette similar to that in the featured quilt, refer to the fabric key below.

Cutting

All measurements include ¼" seam allowances.

From *each* of the 16 prints, cut:
2 squares, 7½" × 7½" (32 total); cut the squares into quarters diagonally to yield 8 small triangles of each color (128 total)

From the navy solid, cut:
2 strips, 12½" × 42"; crosscut into:
    4 squares, 12½" × 12½"; cut the squares in half diagonally to yield 8 large triangles
    2 squares, 12" × 12"
3 strips, 12" × 42"; crosscut *2 of the strips* into:
    2 pieces, 12" × 16"
    2 pieces, 4½" × 12"*
6 strips, 2½" × 42"

*Save the excess strip for the border.

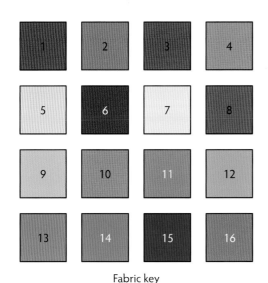

Fabric key

Making the Star

Use a ¼" seam allowance. Press all seam allowances as indicated by the arrows.

1. Working on a design wall or other large surface, arrange the assorted small triangles in a star pattern consisting of whole and half Hourglass blocks, following the suggested layout of fabric numbers if desired. The star should be eight blocks wide and eight blocks tall.

Tech Tip

Use a smartphone or tablet to snap a quick picture of your quilt layout before you start sewing. Besides being a great reference while piecing, it can also help you notice trouble spots with color placement. ↰

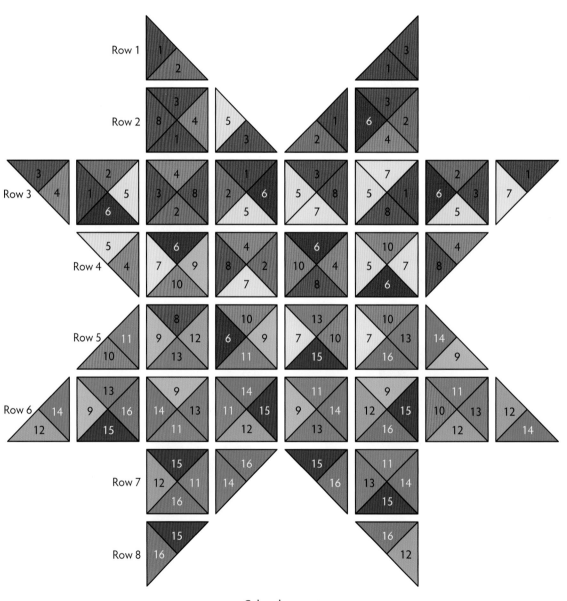

Color placement

2. To piece each Hourglass block, sew small triangles together in pairs along their short edges. Press. Sew the two pairs together. Press. Trim to 6¼" square, including seam allowances. Make 24 Hourglass blocks.

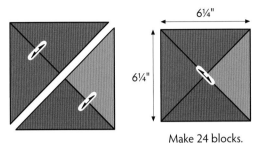

Make 24 blocks.

3. To piece each half block, sew a pair of small triangles together. Press. Make 16 half blocks.

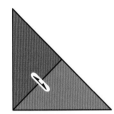

Make 16 half blocks.

4. Trim the half Hourglass blocks to 6⅝" × 6⅝", as if each were a complete square.

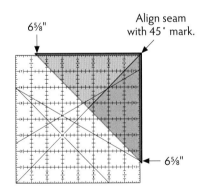

6⅝"

Align seam with 45° mark.

6⅝"

5. Sew the trimmed half blocks to the adjoining full block on each end of rows 2, 3, 6, and 7. Sew a navy large triangle to the diagonal edge of the pieced triangle units. Press, then trim these units to 12" square, including seam allowances.

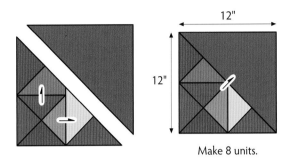

12"

12"

Make 8 units.

Assembling the Quilt Top

1. Sew together a navy 12" square, star point units in rows 1 and 2, and a navy 12" × 16" piece to make the top star section. It should be 12" × 50½", including seam allowances.

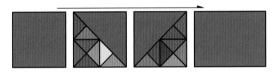

Make 1 top star section, 12" × 50½".

2. Join the center four Hourglass blocks in each of rows 3 and 4. Sew together rows 3 and 4. Join the star point units, joined rows 3 and 4, and a navy 4½" × 12" piece to make the warm middle star section. It should be 12" × 50½", including seam allowances.

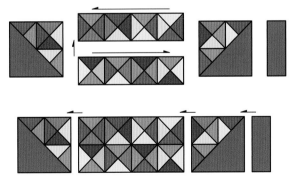

Make 1 warm middle star section, 12" × 50½".

Designed by Diane Brinton and Audrey Mann; pieced and quilted by Diane Brinton

3. Referring to the diagram for pressing directions and block orientation, repeat step 2 to join rows 5 and 6 and make the cool middle star section.

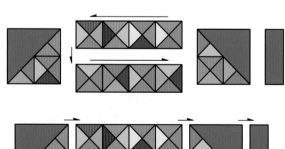

Make 1 cool middle star section,
12" × 50½".

4. Referring to the diagram for pressing directions and block orientation, repeat step 1 to join rows 7 and 8 and make the bottom star section.

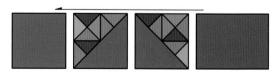

Make 1 bottom star section,
12" × 50½".

5. Join the navy 12" × 42" strip and leftover 12"-wide strip end to end. Trim the strip to 12" × 50½" for the top border.

6. Sew together the top border, top star section, warm and cool middle star sections, and bottom star section to complete the quilt top. The quilt top should be 50½" × 58".

Quilt assembly

Finishing the Quilt

Visit ShopMartingale.com/HowtoQuilt for free downloadable information on the following finishing techniques.

1. Prepare the quilt backing so it is about 6" larger in both directions than the quilt top.

2. Layer the backing, batting, and quilt top. Baste the layers together.

3. Hand or machine quilt as desired. The quilt shown is machine quilted with an allover star pattern in the background and geometric lines in the star.

4. Use the navy 2½"-wide strips to make double-fold binding; attach the binding to the quilt. Add a label if desired.

· Piece & Light ·

Piece & Joy

Celebrate in a big way with this life-size tree set on a white snowy background. We used traditional holiday colors, with wintry blues mixed in for a modern look. Mix solids and prints together to avoid an overly busy look.

FINISHED QUILT: 58½" × 69½" | FINISHED BLOCK: 5¾" × 5¾"

Materials

Yardage is based on 42"-wide fabric.

- 11 squares, 7½" × 7½" each, of assorted green prints and solids for tree 1–10 and 29*

- 10 squares, 7½" × 7½" each, of assorted aqua prints and solids for tree 11–20*

- 9 squares, 7½" × 7½" each, of assorted pink and red prints and solids for tree 21–28 and 30*

- 10 squares, 7½" × 7½" each, of assorted blue prints and solids for tree 31–40*

*Label your fabrics as a color progression when laying out the quilt. For interest, we included lights, mediums, and darks in each color range. If you'd like to use a palette similar to that in the featured quilt, refer to the fabric key below.

- 2⅝ yards of white solid for background
- ⅝ yard of red print for binding
- 3⅝ yards of fabric for backing
- 65" × 76" piece of batting

Cutting

All measurements include ¼" seam allowances.

From each of the assorted print and solid squares:
Cut each 7½" square into quarters diagonally to yield 4 small triangles (160 total)

From the red print, cut:
7 strips, 2½" × 42"

Continued on page 62

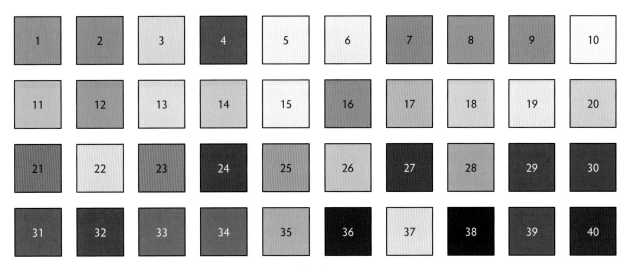

Fabric key

Continued from page 61

From the white solid, cut:

2 strips, 12½" × 42"; crosscut into:

    4 squares, 12½" × 12½"; cut each square in half diagonally to yield 8 large triangles

    2 pieces, 12" × 12½"

5 strips, 12" × 42"; crosscut *3 of the strips* into:

    1 piece, 12" × 29¾"

    1 piece, 12" × 24"

    1 piece, 12" × 18¼"

    1 piece, 12" × 17¾"

    1 square, 12" × 12"

    1 piece, 6¼" × 12"

Making the Tree

Use a ¼" seam allowance. Press all seam allowances as indicated by the arrows.

1. Working on a design wall or other large surface, arrange the assorted print small triangles in a tree pattern consisting of whole and half Hourglass blocks, following the suggested layout of fabric numbers if desired. The tree should be 8 blocks wide and 10 blocks tall.

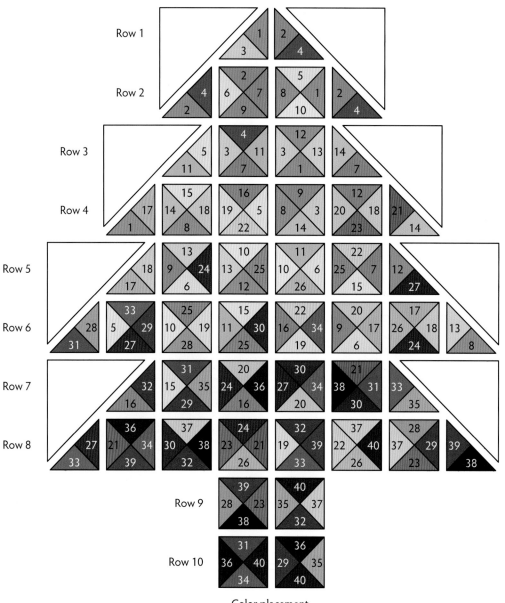

Color placement

Piece & Love

2. To piece each Hourglass block, sew small triangles together in pairs along their short edges. Press. Sew the two pairs together. Press. Trim to 6¼" square, including seam allowances. Make 32 Hourglass blocks.

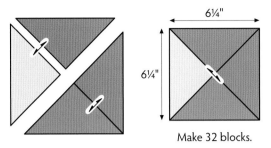

Make 32 blocks.

3. To piece each half block, sew a pair of small triangles together. Press. Make 16 half blocks.

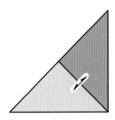

Make 16 half blocks.

4. Trim the half Hourglass blocks to 6⅝" × 6⅝", as if each were a complete square.

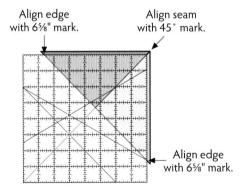

Align edge with 6⅝" mark.

Align seam with 45° mark.

Align edge with 6⅝" mark.

5. Sew the trimmed half blocks to the adjoining full block on both ends of row 2 as shown on page 65. Sew a white large triangle to the diagonal edge of the half-square units to make a tree point unit. Trim to

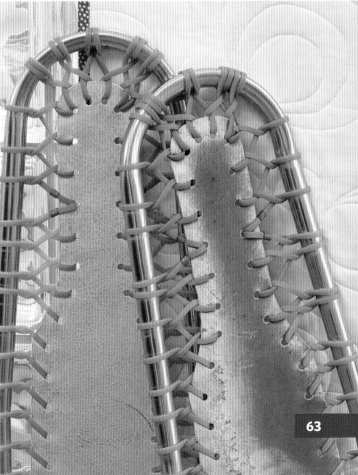

Designed by Diane Brinton and Audrey Mann; pieced by Audrey Mann; quilted by Diane Brinton

·Piece & Love·

12" square, including seam allowances. Repeat for the blocks on each end of rows 4, 6, and 8 to make a total of 8 units.

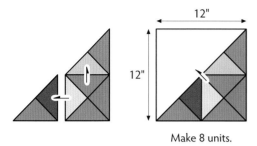

Make 8 units.

6. Sew together a white 12" × 24" piece, two tree point units, and a white 12" square to make the first tree section. It should be 12" × 58½", including seam allowances.

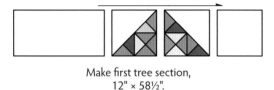

Make first tree section,
12" × 58½".

7. For the second tree section, sew four Hourglass blocks in the middle together in two pairs, then join the pairs. Join a white 12" × 18¼" piece, two tree point units, the middle Hourglass block unit, and a white 6¼" × 12" piece in a row. The second tree section should be 12" × 58½", including seam allowances.

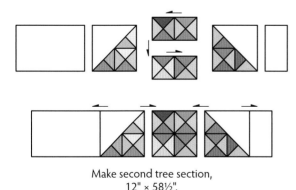

Make second tree section,
12" × 58½".

8. For the third tree section, sew eight Hourglass blocks in the middle together in two rows, then join the rows. Join a white 12" × 12½" piece, two tree

point blocks, and the middle Hourglass block unit in a row. The third tree section should be 12" × 58½", including seam allowances.

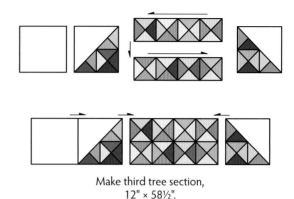

Make third tree section,
12" × 58½".

9. Pressing as shown in the diagram, repeat step 8 to make the fourth tree section.

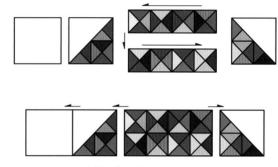

Make fourth tree section,
12" × 58½".

10. For the trunk section, sew four Hourglass blocks in the middle together in two pairs, then join the pairs. Join the white 12" × 29¾" piece, middle Hourglass block unit, and white 12" × 17¾" piece in a row. It should be 12" × 58½", including seam allowances.

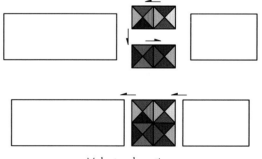

Make trunk section,
12" × 58½".

Assembling the Quilt Top

1. Join the white 12" × 42" strips end to end. Trim the pieced strip to 58½" long for the top border.

2. Sew the top border and tree rows together as shown in the quilt assembly diagram. The quilt top should be 58½" × 69½".

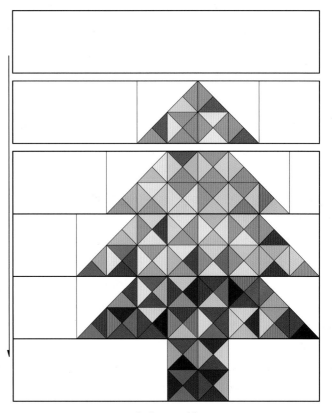

Quilt assembly

Finishing the Quilt

Visit ShopMartingale.com/HowtoQuilt for free downloadable information on the following finishing techniques.

1. Prepare the quilt backing so it is about 6" larger in both directions than the quilt top.

2. Layer the backing, batting, and quilt top. Baste the layers together.

3. Hand or machine quilt as desired. The quilt shown is machine quilted with an allover loop pattern to mimic snowballs.

4. Use the red 2½"-wide strips to make double-fold binding; attach the binding to the quilt. Add a label if desired.

· Piece & Love ·

Piece & Quiet

Spend some time in the mountains gazing at the moon and stars to really find a quiet place. Layered colors give visual depth to the mountain peaks in this on-point beauty.

FINISHED QUILT: 40½" × 50½"

Materials

Yardage is based on 42"-wide fabric. Fat quarters are 18" × 21".

- 1¼ yards of gray tone on tone for background and binding
- 1 fat quarter of white print for moon and stars
- ¼ yard *each* of dark pink, light pink, purple, and dark purple prints for top mountain (4 total)
- ¼ yard *each* of green, light green, olive, turquoise, blue, and dark blue prints for right mountain (6 total)
- ¼ yard *each* of yellow-green, light gold, gold, dark gold, orange, and red prints for bottom mountain (6 total)
- 2¾ yards of fabric for backing
- 47" × 58" piece of batting

Cutting

All measurements include ¼" seam allowances.

From the gray tone on tone, cut:
1 strip, 10⅝" × 42"; crosscut into:
    2 squares, 10⅝" × 10⅝"
    1 strip, 4¼" × 18½"
    1 strip, 4¼" × 18"
2 strips, 4¼" × 42"; crosscut into:
    1 strip, 4¼" × 20½"
    2 strips, 4¼" × 13"
    1 piece, 4¼" × 6¼"
    1 strip, 3" × 10½"
    4 squares, 3" × 3"
5 strips, 2½" × 42"
2 strips, 2" × 42"; crosscut into:
    1 strip, 2" × 12"
    1 strip, 2" × 8¼"
    2 strips, 2" × 7½"
    1 piece, 2" × 6½"
    1 piece, 2" × 5¾"
    1 piece, 2" × 4¼"
    1 piece, 2" × 2¾"

From the white print, cut:
1 square, 10½" × 10½"
6 squares, 2" × 2"

From the dark pink print, cut:
1 strip, 5½" × 28½"

From the light pink print, cut:
1 strip, 5½" × 33½"

Continued on page 69

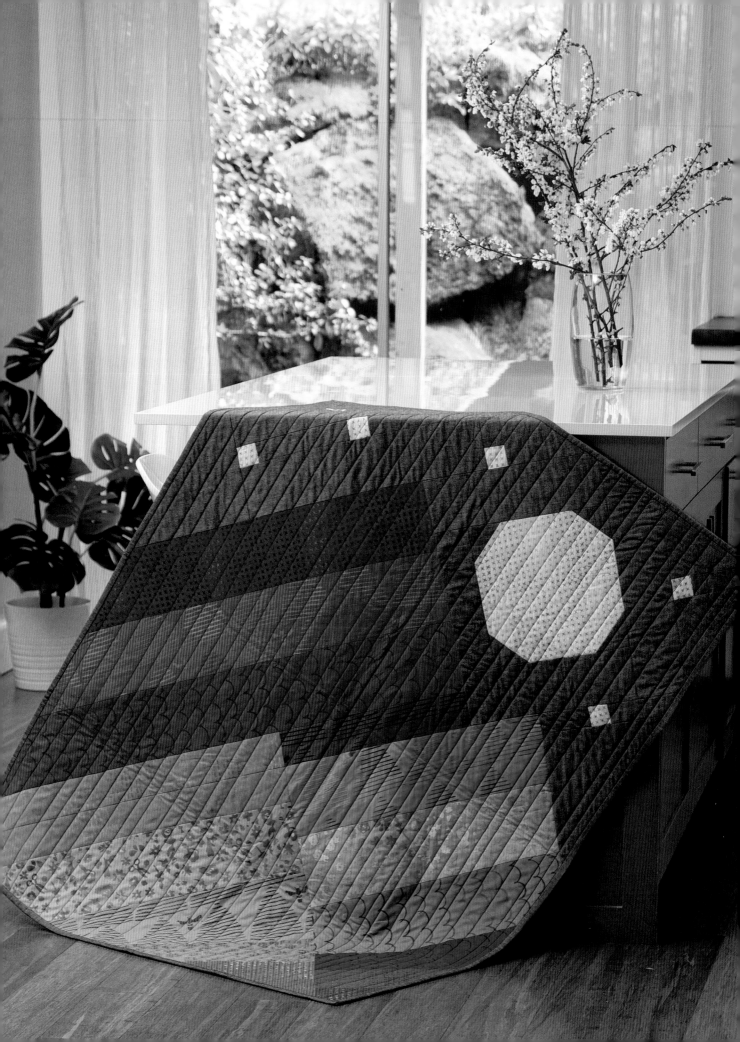

Continued from page 67

From the purple print, cut:
1 strip, 5½" × 38½"

From the dark purple print, cut:
1 strip, 3" × 14½"

From the green print, cut:
1 strip, 5½" × 19½"

From the light green print, cut:
1 strip, 5½" × 19½"

From the olive print, cut:
1 strip, 5½" × 19½"

From the turquoise print, cut:
1 strip, 5½" × 15¾"

From the blue print, cut:
1 strip, 5½" × 10¾"

From the dark blue print, cut:
1 piece, 4½" × 5¾"

From the yellow-green print, cut:
2 strips, 3" × 42"; crosscut into 2 strips, 3" × 27½"

From the light gold print, cut:
1 strip, 5½" × 25½"

From the gold print, cut:
1 strip, 5½" × 20½"

From the dark gold print, cut:
1 strip, 5½" × 15½"

From the orange print, cut:
1 strip, 5½" × 10½"

From the red print, cut:
1 square, 5½" × 5½"

Making the Left Sky Section

Use a ¼" seam allowance. Press all seam allowances as indicated by the arrows.

1. Sew together a gray 2" × 7½" strip, a white 2" square, and a gray 2" × 8¼" strip as shown to make row 1. In same manner, join two white 2" squares, a gray 2" × 7½" strip, and a gray 2" × 12" strip to make

row 3. Sew together a gray 2" × 2¾" piece and a white 2" square. Add a gray 4¼" × 18½" strip to the left side and a gray 4¼" × 6¼" piece to the right side to make row 4. Aligning the left edges, join the rows with a gray 4¼" × 20½" strip for row 2.

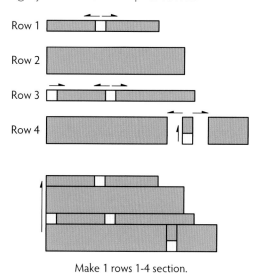

Make 1 rows 1-4 section.

2. Cut one gray 10⅝" square in half diagonally to make two A triangles.

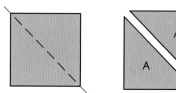

3. Fold one gray A triangle in half and crease the center; unfold. Matching the crease mark with the center of the white square in row 1, join the triangle and the rows from step 1. Matching the bottom edges, sew the remaining gray A triangle to the left edge of the rows to make the left sky section.

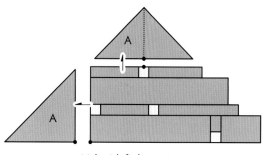

Make 1 left sky section.

Making the Moon and Top Mountain Section

1. Draw a diagonal line on the wrong side of each gray 3" square. Place a marked square right sides together on each corner of the white 10½" square. Sew along the diagonal lines, then trim the corners ¼" from the seams. Press the gray triangles open.

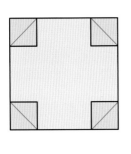 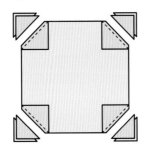

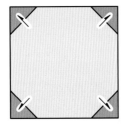

Make 1 unit,
10½" × 10½".

2. Sew the gray 3" × 10½" strip to the left side of the block from step 1. Sew gray 4¼" × 13" strips to the top and bottom edges of the block, then add the gray 4¼" × 18" strip to the right side. The Moon block should be 16¾" × 18", including seam allowances.

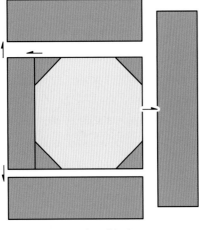

Make 1 block,
16¾" × 18".

3. Cut the remaining gray 10⅝" square in half diagonally to make two A triangles. Cut one A triangle in half as shown to make two B triangles.

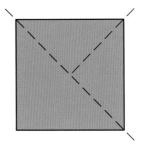 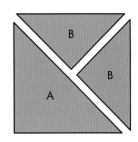

4. Sew a white 2" square to the gray 2" × 5¾" piece, then sew the gray B triangles to the top and bottom, aligning the left edges.

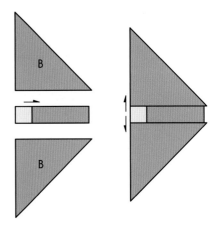

5. On the right edge of the Moon block, make a mark 7½" from the bottom edge. Match and pin this marked point to the center of the white 2" square on the unit from step 4. Join the pieces to make the moon section.

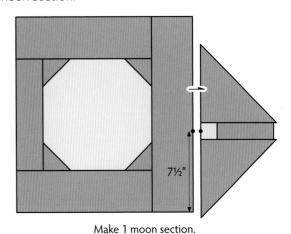

7½"

Make 1 moon section.

·Piece & Love·

Designed by Diane Brinton and Audrey Mann; pieced by Audrey Mann; quilted by Diane Brinton

6. Sew the dark purple 3" × 14½" strip and one yellow-green 3" × 27½" strip together end to end. Aligning the right edges, sew the dark pink, light pink, purple, and yellow-green/dark purple pieces together to make the top mountain section.

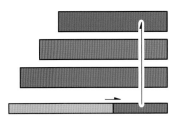

Make 1 top mountain section.

7. Join the top mountain section to the moon section.

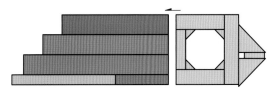

Make 1 top mountain/moon section.

Making the Bottom Mountain Section

1. Sew a gray 2" × 4¼" piece, white 2" square, and gray 2" × 6½" piece together in a row. Sew the remaining gray A triangle to the bottom edge, aligning the left edges.

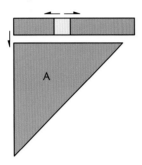

2. Aligning the left edges, sew the green, light green, olive, turquoise, blue, and dark blue strips together to make the right mountain section.

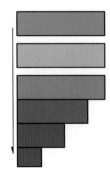

Make 1 right mountain section.

3. Aligning the right edges, sew the yellow-green 3" × 27½" strip; light gold, gold, dark gold, and orange strips; and the red square together.

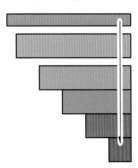

4. Aligning their top edges, sew the units from steps 1–3 together to make the bottom mountain section.

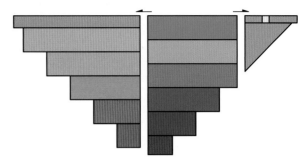

Make 1 bottom mountain section.

Assembling the Quilt Top

1. On the top edge of the Moon block, make a mark 4¼" from the right edge. Match and pin this marked point to the right edge of the left sky section, then sew together. Align the left edges of the top mountain and bottom mountain sections, making sure that the two yellow-green pieces are lined up at the seams, then sew together.

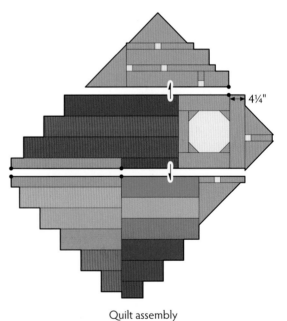

Quilt assembly

2. Using a long straight ruler for top and side edges and a square ruler for corners, trim the top edge of the quilt even with the upper-left triangle. Trim the sides and bottom edge even with where the

· Piece & Love ·

mountain strips overlap. Handle the quilt top carefully, as most of the edges are cut on the bias and could stretch out of shape. Baste ⅛" from the edge all the way around the quilt-top perimeter to prevent stretching. The quilt top should be 40½" × 50½".

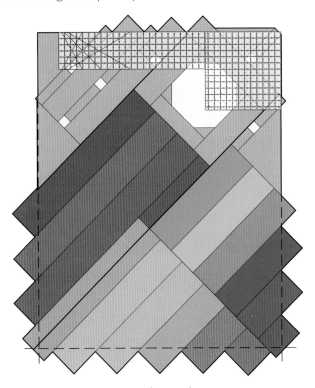

Trim quilt-top edges.

Finishing the Quilt

For more details on any finishing steps, visit ShopMartingale.com/HowtoQuilt for free downloadable information.

1. Prepare the quilt backing so it is about 6" larger in both directions than the quilt top.

2. Layer the backing, batting, and quilt top. Baste the layers together.

3. Hand or machine quilt as desired. The quilt shown is quilted with parallel vertical straight lines.

4. Use the gray 2½"-wide strips to make double-fold binding; attach the binding to the quilt. Add a label if desired.

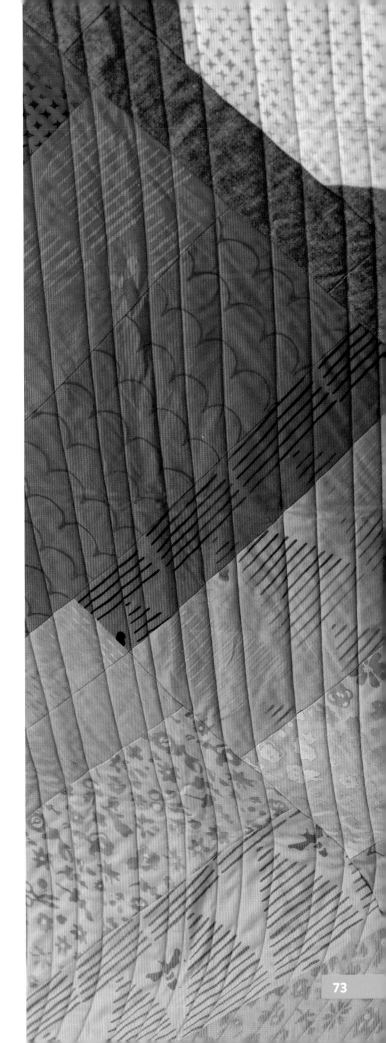

Paint Box

Who doesn't love a brand-spanking-new box of paints? Use all the colors of the rainbow to get your creative juices flowing, and reminisce about that first day of school with fresh new supplies. A little bit of paper-foundation piecing makes this paintbrush look authentic.

FINISHED QUILT: 46½" × 24½"

Materials

Yardage is based on 42"-wide fabric.

- 4 squares, 5" × 5", of assorted tone on tones for paints (1 *each* of pink, green, grass green, and dark pink)
- 12 squares, 10" × 10", of assorted tone on tones for paints (1 *each* of lavender, purple, dark blue, blue, light blue, turquoise, lime, yellow, dark yellow, orange, dark orange, and red)
- ⅛ yard of charcoal tone on tone for brush handle
- 3" × 4" piece of gold tone on tone for brush ferrule
- 3" × 6" piece of black tone on tone for paintbrush tip
- 1 yard of light gray solid for background
- ⅜ yard of dark pink solid for binding
- 1½ yards of fabric for backing
- 31" × 53" piece of batting

Cutting

All measurements include ¼" seam allowances.

From *each* of the assorted print 5" × 5" squares, cut:
3 squares, 2½" × 2½"

From *each* of the assorted print 10" × 10" squares, cut:
6 squares, 2½" × 2½"

From the charcoal tone on tone, cut:
1 strip, 2½" × 32½"

From the light gray solid, cut:
4 strips, 3½" × 42"; crosscut into:
   2 strips, 3½" × 40½"
   2 strips, 3½" × 24½" (Save leftover fabric for paper piecing.)
5 strips, 2½" × 42"; crosscut into:
   2 strips, 2½" × 40½"
   12 pieces, 2½" × 6½"
   1 square, 2½" × 2½"
2 strips, 1¼" × 42"; crosscut into 56 squares, 1¼" × 1¼"

From the dark pink solid, cut:
Enough 2½"-wide bias strips to total 150"

Making the Paints

Use a ¼" seam allowance. Press all seam allowances as indicated by the arrows.

1. Lay out three pink and three lavender 2½" squares in three rows, alternating colors. Join the rows to make a pink/lavender six-patch unit measuring 4½" × 6½", including seam allowances.

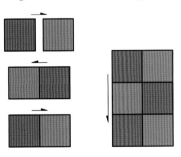

Make 1 pink/lavender unit, 4½" × 6½".

2. Using the pairs of colors listed below, repeat step 1 to make 13 additional six-patch units:

- lavender/purple
- purple/dark blue
- dark blue/blue
- blue/light blue
- light blue/turquoise
- turquoise/green
- grass green/lime
- lime/yellow
- yellow/dark yellow
- dark yellow/orange
- orange/dark orange
- dark orange/red
- red/dark pink

Lavender/ purple   Purple/ dark blue   Dark blue/ blue   Blue/ light blue

Light blue/ turquoise   Turquoise/ green   Grass green/ lime

Lime/ yellow   Yellow/ dark yellow   Dark yellow/ orange

Orange/ dark orange   Dark orange/ red   Red/ dark pink

Make 1 of each unit,
4½" × 6½".

3. Draw a diagonal line on the wrong side of each light gray 1¼" square. Place a marked square in each corner of a six-patch block, right sides together. Sew on the diagonal lines, then trim the corners ¼" from the seams. The Paint block should be 4½" × 6½", including seam allowances. Make 14 Paint blocks.

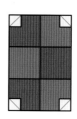 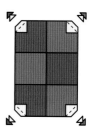

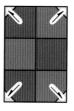

Make 14 blocks,
4½" × 6½".

4. Sew together the seven cool Paint blocks alternately with six light gray 2½" × 6½" pieces to make the cool paint row. Use the remaining Paint blocks and six light gray 2½" × 6½" pieces to make the warm paint row. Each row should be 6½" × 40½", including seam allowances.

Make 1 cool row,
6½" × 40½".

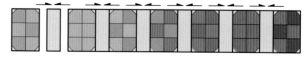

Make 1 warm row,
6½" × 40½".

· *Piece & Love* ·

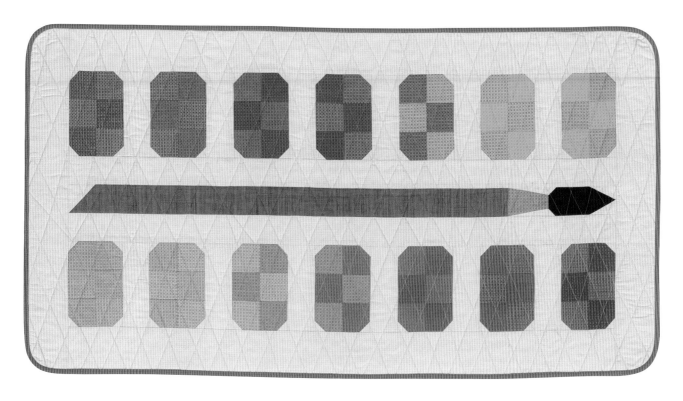

Designed by Diane Brinton and Audrey Mann; pieced and quilted by Audrey Mann

Making the Paintbrush

1. Draw a diagonal line on the wrong side of the light gray 2½" square. Place the marked square on one end of the charcoal 2½" × 32½" strip, right sides together. Sew on the diagonal line and trim the corner ¼" from the seam. Press the resulting triangle open to make the paintbrush handle. It should be 2½" × 32½", including seam allowances.

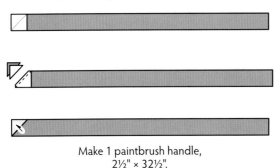

Make 1 paintbrush handle,
2½" × 32½".

2. The ferrule and brush tip are both paper-foundation pieced. Make paper copies of the patterns on page 79 to piece these units. Using the gold piece and leftover light gray solid, paper piece the brush ferrule. For a more detailed explanation about paper foundation piecing, go to ShopMartingale.com/HowtoQuilt for free downloadable instructions. The brush ferrule should be 2½" × 3½", including seam allowances.

Make 1 brush ferrule,
2½" × 3½".

3. Using the black piece and leftover light gray solid, paper piece the brush tip. It should be 2½" × 5½", including seam allowances.

Make 1 brush tip,
2½" × 5½".

·Paint Box·

4. Sew the brush handle, ferrule, and tip together to make the paintbrush. It should be 2½" × 40½", including seam allowances.

Make 1 paintbrush, 2½" × 40½".

Assembling the Quilt Top

Lay out the following pieces in rows as shown: a light gray 3½" × 40½" border strip, the cool paint row, a light gray 2½" × 40½" sashing strip, the paintbrush, a light gray 2½" × 40½" sashing strip, the warm paint row, and a light gray 3½" × 40½" border strip. Join the rows. Sew a light gray 3½" × 24½" border strip to each end to complete the quilt top. The quilt top should be 46½" × 24½".

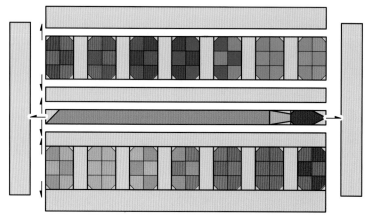

Quilt assembly

Finishing the Quilt

Visit ShopMartingale.com/HowtoQuilt for free downloadable information on the following finishing techniques.

1. Prepare the quilt backing so it is about 6" larger in both directions than the quilt top.

2. Layer the backing, batting, and quilt top. Baste the layers together.

3. Hand or machine quilt as desired. The quilt shown is machine quilted with a diamond-shaped crosshatching. If desired, use the curved corner template (page 79) to round the corners of the quilt sandwich before binding to emulate the look of a child's paintbox.

4. Use the dark pink 2½"-wide bias strips to make double-fold binding; attach the binding to the quilt. Add a label if desired.

· Piece & Love ·

Paint Box brush tip

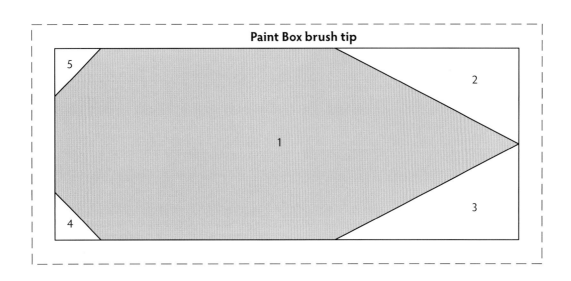

5
2
1
4
3

Paint Box brush ferrule

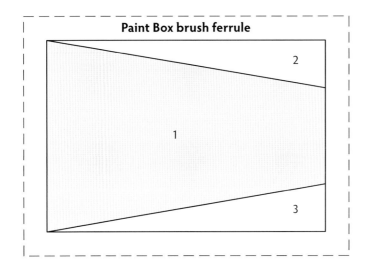

2
1
3

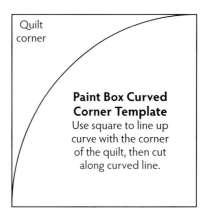

Quilt corner

Paint Box Curved Corner Template
Use square to line up curve with the corner of the quilt, then cut along curved line.

About the Authors

Diane Brinton and Audrey Mann have been a mother-daughter creative team since 2012. They run the Cloth Parcel, an online pattern shop and blog, where mom Diane and daughter Audrey put their combined decades of experience in sewing, quilting, and design to use. They have written more than 50 patterns for the Cloth Parcel, and their work has been published in multiple magazines and books. Find them online at TheClothParcel.com.

Diane began sewing her own clothing in fourth grade and never looked back. She discovered quilting in 1999, so she could send a quilt to college with her oldest daughter. Since then, she's made hundreds of quilts, including intricate hand-appliqué masterpieces. Diane is a wife, mom, and grandma. She loves all things art and design and has a bachelor of arts degree from Brigham Young University.

Audrey wasn't very interested in sewing or quilting until she had a family of her own and found a supply of modern fabrics that were to her liking. Once she realized sewing didn't have to look like something from pioneer days, a whole new world opened up. She is a wife, and mom to four children. She also enjoys art, lettering, and illustration and has a bachelor of science degree from Utah State University.